Religion & Sexuality

Judaic-Christian Viewpoints in the USA

Monograph #1

Edited by
John M. Holland, Ph.D.

The Association of Sexologists

Copyright © 1981 by The Association of Sexologists.
All Rights Reserved.

Printed in the U.S.A.

Library of Congress Catalog Card No.: 81-66867

ISBN: 0-939902-00-1

The Association of Sexologists
1523 Franklin St.
San Francisco, CA 94109, USA

TABLE OF CONTENTS

Chapter One
INTRODUCTION 1
    John M. Holland, Ph.D., Member of the Organizing Cadre of the Association of Sexologists, Former Director of Education, Human Sexuality Program, University of California, San Francisco, Calif.

Chapter Two
JEWISH VIEWS OF SEXUALITY 6
    Allen Bennett, M.H.L., Rabbi, Congregation Sha'ar Zahzu, San Francisco; Co-chair, Council on Religion and the Homosexual, San Francisco, Calif.

Chapter Three
ROMAN CATHOLIC VIEWS OF SEXUALITY . . . 18
    James H. Schulte, Ph.D., Co-author of *Human Sexuality, New Directions in American Catholic Thought*, N.Y.: Paulist, 1977.

Chapter Four
PROTESTANT VIEWS OF SEXUALITY 32
    Letha Scanzoni, B.A., Full-time professional writer, specializing in social issues and religion, recently co-authored *Is the Homosexual My Neighbor?: Another Christian View* (with Virginia Ramey Mollenkott), N.Y.: Harper and Row, 1978.

Chapter Five
TOWARD A THEOLOGY OF HUMAN SEXUALITY . 49
    James B. Nelson, Ph.D., Professor, Christian Ethics United Theological Seminary of the Twin Cities, New Brighton, Minn.; Minister of United Church of Christ; author of *Embodiment: An Approach to Sexuality and Christian Theology*, Augsburg Press, 1978.

Chapter Six
AFTERWORD 64
    William Simon, Ph.D., A.C.S., Professor of Sociology, University of Houston, Houston, Texas; eminent sex researcher and author in the field of sexology.

ACKNOWLEDGMENTS

This monograph is the first in a series of professional and semi-professional editions contributing to the field of Sexology. Through sponsorship of these publications, The Association of Sexologists seeks to encourage and increase the flow of credible and useable information in the area of sexuality. Therefore, it is appropriate that I first thank the members of The Association of Sexologists who support this and other important tasks in our field.

I appreciate the efforts made by James Nelson, Letha Scanzoni, and James Schulte for submitting manuscripts of presentations prepared for a conference on the same topic. My thanks also go to Allen Bennett who responded to a last minute request for a manuscript and to Bill Simon for his willingness to provide an afterword.

I'm personally grateful to Stephen LaPorta, whose editorial assistance provides a more readable text and made the overall work of editing bearable. My wife Catrinka Smirl, companion-critic, helped me eliminate much of my own judgmentalness and provided both affection and patience in support of this project. Dick Ellington, in addition to being typographer, dispelled the myths of publication with wise guidance and a dedication to the principles of freedom of the press.

Nothing could have been created without my fellow Association staff. Mickey Apter gave constant encouragement and Louie Durham dreamed the monograph dream and provided the financial advance which insured the publication of this monograph.

—John M. Holland

PREFACE

Marsilo Ficino, a seventeenth century Italian scholar, was a student of the ways people are religious. His response after years of studying and discovering the many modes people use to sense and express their religious life was summarized in this statement:

> Perhaps indeed variety of this kind,
> divinely ordained, decorates the universe
> with a certain marvelous beauty.
> (Smith, 1964)

I have a similar poetic response to my own exploration of the many ways people sense and express their sexuality. During my ten years in the sex field I have developed a spirited appreciation for the diversity by which human individuals are sexual.

The other writers in this monograph share with me the observation that a variety of sexual viewpoints exist in this society and its religious communities; and this multiformity "decorates the universe with a certain marvelous beauty."

—John M. Holland

Chapter One
INTRODUCTION

John M. Holland, Ph.D.

The predominant mood in the United States toward sexual attitudes and behaviors has become more relaxed and less charged with emotion during the last 20 years. Individuals are reexamining their ideas about sexuality. There is also a growing sentiment, even in puritanical segments of America, that suggests each person has the right to enjoy the physical and psychological pleasures (Albee, 1977, p. 160) that may flow from their own sexuality. The conspiracy of silence which permeated sexual matters has faded. Today people are more able to inquire about their own sexual functioning and the sexual aspects of their relationships. Articles on sexual topics are discussed in most popular magazines and books. Currently, nineteen professional periodicals are devoted solely to the topic of sexuality.

As a result of these changing attitudes, more individuals in our society feel free to seek counsel about their sexuality. Indeed, they expect and deserve a competent response. Some people, however, remain uneasy about directly discussing sexual matters. They often seek out professional help, often from their minister or rabbi, to confide about their sexuality. Unfortunately, over-reaction, indifference and moralistic judgments often characterize the responses helping professionals give when sexuality is discussed. If we explore some of the origins of the prevailing sexual attitudes of Western culture, we can realize how these views influence the sexual ideologies of clergy and laypersons alike.

The Judaic-Christian tradition viewed sex as a primarily reproductive function. For the early Hebrews, the function of sex was to propagate the family lineage and the Hebrew people. Christianity shared this procreative bias and believed that sexual activity should be limited to married and fertile heterosexuals. Roman Catholic doctrine influenced by Thomas Acquinas insisted that sexuality conform to the laws of "nature" (Haeberle, 1978, p. 323).

Medieval Christianity elevated chastity to a supreme spiritual position—even over marriage. The Reformers, such as Luther and Calvin, reinforced the sex for reproduction bias, but did not regard sexual abstinence as being more spiritual than marriage. There was little toleration, however, for sexual activity outside of marriage, or sexual activity among married couples that was considered "unnatural" or nonreproductive in purpose. The Protestants of the New World managed to get many of their sexual mores legislated into penal codes. Common sex behavior such as oral sex, even between married or consenting adults, was considered a criminal offense against God and "nature." Currently, many states maintain some of these laws on the books, although enforcement is sporadic and arbitrary.

Victorianism was the dominant sexual theory during the last half of the nineteenth century. Sexual activity was believed to threaten moral character and drain vital energy (Robinson, 1977, Chap. 1). This viewpoint was primarily influential in England and America; consequently, sexuality was held in suspicion, and sexual feelings and sexual information were generally suppressed (Brecker, 1969, Intro.).

In regard to sexual attitudes, religious influence upon the scientific community was greatly reduced with the introduction of Charles Darwin's evolutionary theory in the nineteenth century. Sex for procreation was still maintained as a "natural law"; however, more credence was given to studying sexual behavior because humans were thought to have direct biological connection to other animals. Several influential physicians, however, retained a rigid ideological position on sexuality and regarded nonreproductive sexual activity as "pathological" or "sick" (Krafft-Ebbing, 1898, Chap. 1). This pathological view also influenced civil law in the United States so that sexual acts such as homosexuality, anal sex and sex with animals continued to be viewed as "crimes against nature and society."

The socio-cultural climate of fear and suspicion regarding sexuality was reinforced by ignorance and a religious philosophy which limited sex solely to reproduction and marriage.

During the first half of this century, many changes contributed to bringing sexuality into public awareness. Two world wars, improved global transportation and resulting cultural exchange, transcontinental communications systems, and labor-saving technology all accelerated this process. The creation of metropolitan centers and the major population shift from rural to urban areas greatly affected the familial and small community controls upon individual thinking and attitudes toward sex (Reiss, 1977, p. 312).

Almost every religious body deemed it important to reexamine their position on sexual ethics following the catalysis of the '60s. This was the first major change in almost 2,000 years of Christianity. Approaches to ethical issues throughout the society tended to be less legalistic and more "situational" (Fletcher, 1964).

Issues surrounding the ordination of women and persons whose sexual orientation was homosexual and who were candidates for the office of clergy/ministry, forced many churches to deal with the overall topic of sexuality. Some religious individuals feel reexamination of sexual ethics is neither needed nor beneficial and consider the pluralistic viewpoints of our society toward sexuality as a threat to the moral fiber of this nation (Keating, 1970). Several coalitions have been formed whereby the more "conservative" minded people can voice their views in a style consistent with religious revivals which occurred periodically in our nation's history—when fundamental Protestantism was a dominating political power. This is illustrated in the following statement:

> . . . the future United States was settled and to a large degree shaped by those who brought with them a very special form of radical Protestantism which combined a strenuous moral precisionism, a deep commitment to evangelical experientialism, and a determination to make the state responsible for the support of those

moral and religious ideas. The U.S. became, therefore, the land par excellence of revivalism, moral "legalism" and a "gospel" of work that was undergirded by the so-called Puritan Ethic. (Ahlstrum, 1973, p. 1090)

A drawback I sense in these primarily Fundamental Christian movements, is the inclination to claim the authority to know what is morally "right" for all people.

Many of us in the field of sexology appeal to each segment of our society and its religious communities to recognize and acknowledge the multiplicity of sexual attitudes and behaviors evident throughout our society. Furthermore, we support sexual individuality and seek ways to assist people in the management of their sexuality in ways they feel is more suitable to them personally and socially (Money and Musaph, 1977).

Each of the authors in the subsequent chapters provide us with the content of the various sexual attitudes found in their religious traditions and some projections of a possible theology of human sexuality. The concluding chapter provides a secular viewpoint and response to these expositions. It is our hope as contributors that this monograph will provide more understanding and appreciation of our own and our neighbors' sexuality.

BIBLIOGRAPHY

Ahlstrom, Sidney E., *A Religious History of the American People.* New Haven and London: Yale University Press, 1973.
Albee, G., "The Protestant Ethic, Sex and Psychotherapy," *American Psychologist.* February 1977.
Brecher, E. *The Sex Researchers.* Boston: Little, Brown & Co., 1969.
Fletcher, J. *Situational Ethics.* Philadelphia, Penn.: Westminster Press, 1964.
Haeberle, E. *The Sex Atlas.* New York: Seabury Press, 1978.
Keating, Charles Jr. *Report of the Commission on Obscenity and Pornography.* New York: Bantam Books, 1970.
Krafft-Ebbing, R. V. *Psychopathia Sexualis,* "Antipathic Sexual Instinct, A Medico-Forensic Study" (only authorized English adaptation of the Twelfth German Edition by F. J. Rebman). New York: Medical Art Agency, 1918.
Money, J. and Musaph H. *Handbook of Sexology.* New York: Excerpta Medica, 1977.

Popper, K. *The Open Society and Its Enemies, 2 Hegel and Marx.* Princeton, N.J.: Princeton University Press, 1966.

Reiss, I. "Our Changing Socio Sexual Mores," *Handbook of Sexology.* Amsterdam: Elsevier Medical Press, 1977.

Robinson, P. *The Modernization of Sex.* New York: Harper & Row, 1977.

Smith, Wilfred C. *The Meaning and End of Religion, A New Approach to the Religious Tradition of Mankind.* New York: Mentor, 1964.

Chapter Two
JEWISH VIEWS OF SEXUALITY

Allen B. Bennett, M.H.L., Rabbi

Introduction

Jewish tradition, historically, has always maintained that where there are two Jews, there will be three opinions. Said knowingly and with a twinkle in the eye, this axiom helps to explain the vast range of attitudes and legal positions which various "Judaisms" have expressed over the centuries on every conceivable subject. Human sexuality was certainly no exception. And what follows is an overview of some of the general attitudes held at various times by various segments of the Jewish community with regard to sexuality.

Concepts related to human sexuality have run the gamut in Judaism, from conservative, almost ascetic philosophies, to the most contemporary, liberal views. This has been true throughout Jewish history, and there have even been times where diametrically opposed positions were in vogue at the same time. The whole panoply of human emotions has been played out in the Jewish literature on the subject of human sexuality and sensuality. Topics as predictable as sexual intercourse have had full coverage, with volumes written on procedures and policies, and topics as exotic as the legally bigamous marriage of one man to two sisters have been discussed as well.

Biblical Views

It should be noted that in Judaism the term Bible refers solely to what is referred to in Christianity as the Old Testament. Any reference to the Bible in this paper is made with that understanding.

To begin an examination of Biblical views of sexuality, one must put the whole issue of legislating human behavior into a proper context. In her book on Women and Judaism, Roslyn Lacks states:

> Laws of a community more often reflect its ideals rather than its practices. Prohibitions against certain acts would obviously be unnecessary if proscribed behaviors did not occur. Leviticus 18:18, by way of example, forbids marriage and intercourse with two sisters; yet the story of the twelve tribes of Israel emanates from just such a union between Jacob and the sisters Rachel and Leah. The human sexual drive, subject to regulation in all communities, often finds ways of circumventing prohibitions placed upon it. This very ingenuity accounts, in part, for divergent attitudes toward sexuality in Biblical text. While sensuality is clearly celebrated in the Song of Songs, sexuality is stringently circumscribed in the legal codes. Levitical law makes no issue of virginity; later Deuteronomic legislation emphatically demands it. (Lacks, 1980, p. 115)

By examining the social situation of the ancient Hebrews, one can gain insight into attempts to control human sexuality. The Jews of the First Commonwealth, i.e., up to the destruction of the Temple in 586 B.C.E., viewed sexual matters quite simply. Stable family life was the critical issue; a smooth and comfortable relationship between the sexes was seen as the basis for this stability. Men and women were perceived as mutually interdependent; it was believed that a man discovers himself only through contact with a woman. By virtue of becoming one flesh and deriving from one flesh, men and women were led to the building of the family, which was seen as the foundation of a humane society. The purpose of sexuality was thus to propagate the species through the creation of a family.

Biblical sexual morality was less complex than that of the later Jewish legal codes. Yet it contained some interesting features, all geared to the stability of the family and the community. One important area was the lack of an antisexual or ascetic tradition, which later came into existence in Greek and Christian thought. And as would be expected in a patriarchal society, men had more rights, but women were acknowledged as people and their rights were considered at the same time. Even polygamy, which was practiced throughout the Biblical period by rich or important men, was a crucial source of solidarity as it provided that every woman would have some kind of family structure to belong to.

In the period of the Second Commonwealth (586 B.C.E. to 70 C.E.), standards of sex morality changed radically. The first trend to influence the family was urbanization and the development of a commercial society. Contact with other nations increased, commerce sprouted up in Judea, and the transition from an agricultural peasant community into a commercial city-dwelling community began. With urbanization came an increase in alienation from tribal mores and moral boundaries, creating a greater need for institutions to restrain and limit the activity of people. It was in this setting that a new concept of man developed which held that man is weak and overwhelmed by impulses which frequently overcome him. This, in turn, led to the notion of the evil within man, and the sexual drive was seen as a manifestation of this.

Talmudic Views

By the time of the Talmudic period, the rabbis viewed women as less dangerous than they had been considered during the Second Commonwealth. Social freedom being to an extent rediscovered (along with a more humanitarian outlook), was opposed to asceticism and considered the flesh to be evil only through corruption. A major philosophical concept of this period was that of the *yetzer ha-ra*, the evil inclination. A part of this urge to evil was seen as the sexual drive, which was the source of energy for properly sublimated activities. In other words, man was capable of controlling his passions. Moderation became the watchword of the era. Also, at this time marriage was re-emphasized as an institution of paramount importance.

Post-Talmudic Views

Another shift in attitudes occurred during the post-Talmudic period. Other civilizations exerted an influence on the Jews, and at this time an ascetic strain was introduced into Jewish laws and customs. This period also saw the rise of the medieval concept of dualism, the body-soul dichotomy in which the body was evil and the soul was good. As a result, the moralistic view of this period required a life more disciplined than the law demanded. Since people were seen as part animal and part divine—their sexual appetites being their animal nature and their soul as their divine parts—these aspects were seen to be in constant conflict. Again, the concept of the mastery of our bestial side gained favor, with the understanding that by so doing, one could reach a higher plane of earthly existence.

At the same time it remained evident that one's bodily needs had to be satisfied. If one managed these needs in a satisfactory way, in moderation and not as an end in themselves, one could concentrate his efforts in the exercise of reason, thereby obtaining divinity.

This attitude found its clearest expression in the writings of the Rambam, Rabbi Moses ben Maimon, also known as Maimonides, who wrote that "the most harmonious state is one that shuns the sensuous and sensual, to which all men of superior sense and sensibility can testify" (Lacks, 1980, p. 2).

Contemporaneous with this view in the Middle Ages came the kabbalistic or mystical view of sexual activity, which held that there was something holy and divine about sexual relations.

> It was believed that when a man cleaves to his wife in holiness the Divine Presence is manifested. The cabbalistic view of spirituality was emotional rather than rational. The human body and its physical needs were seen as the manifestation of holiness. Man was seen as the expression of the universal union of the physical and the spiritual. (Epstein, 1967, p. xi)

A medieval Jewish classic on sexual morality, the *Iggeret Ha'Kodesh* ("Holy Letter"), strongly opposes the Maimonidean view of sex, and discusses the sexual relationship of husband and wife with a delicacy that calls to mind the I-Thou relationship described by the late Martin Buber. On an esoteric level, it is also a kabbalistic work depicting God's relationship to His people.

Kabbalistic doctrine regarded physical needs as worthy and good and part of God's manifestation in the finite world. The kabbalist sees the sexual impulse not as a passion to be suppressed, but as a holy urge, natural and noble, with its highest form of expression as the loving union between husband and wife.

One can understand from this brief historical overview that Judaism more or less consistently viewed sexuality as noble and good. Although there were slight differences in some particular aspects in the different periods, sexuality was always perceived as related to the family, to love and to mutuality. Judaism recognized both the biological and the sociological sides of sexuality, accepted them both, and tried to synthesize them into an ethical system that was also practical in its time.

Much was written at this time about the problem of temptation. While Christianity had reached the point where it was promoting the antinomian position—that is, that faith alone was sufficient to obtain salvation—Judaism believed that there were objective standards by which one should live, and that adherence to a moral law was at least as important as faith. For that reason, sexual life was regulated by rules and restrictions, not left to sentiment or subjective feeling. A weak person, overcome by temptation, was not to be stigmatized forever. A hallmark of Judaism was the concept that there was always room for repentance and renewal.

By this time in history, even though there had been centuries of influence from outside sources, certain fundamental themes had become constant in Jewish sex laws and customs. Even today they have not changed much, at least not in traditional or Orthodox Jewish circles. Adultery, rape, prostitution and homosexuality had been severely condemned. And sexual activity outside of marriage was prohibited. Masturbation was viewed as a form of coitus interruptus and was considered to be wasting the seed and was therefore prohibited. Homosexuality was endemic in the Roman Hellenistic civilization, but was considered tabu among the Jews. It was considered a sickness by many, while others suggested that it stemmed from a misdirection of energy which could respond favorably to counseling.

Since it is clear that marriage is the only context in which sexuality was to be expressed (from Biblical through the post-Talmudic period), perhaps it would be appropriate to compare marriage in ancient times with marriage in the modern, industrial world.

> Marriage took place at a much younger age and was more highly regulated and linked to other institutions than in the contemporary world, where people are much less in touch with the rules and regulations pertaining to proper conduct, and where there are fewer social sanctions to keep people in line. Marriage and the family in ancient times involved not only emotional ties but also mutually shared values, sentiments and activities, which undoubtedly contributed to far less strain than exists for the modern family, which is founded and persists on the basis of intense personal relationships unsupported by common activities and clearly defined goals. (Epstein, 1967, p. xiii)

Furthermore,

> With customs and prescribed patterns of behavior well outlined, individuals, in the ancient marriage, had fewer decisions to make then the modern individual, whose greater personal responsibility for his own destiny and decisions makes for greater psychological stress in interpersonal relationships. (Epstein, 1967, p. xiv)

Another factor which helped stabilize things in antiquity was the extended family, which provided emotional support and the opportunity for more secure personal relationships.

> Sexual relationships were less significantly a barometer of interpersonal interfamilial relationships than they are today; they were for procreation and the perpetuation of the community, which, in turn, had a great investment in the proper regulation of sexual habits and behavior. (Epstein, 1967, p. xiv)

Modern Orthodox Views

Modern Orthdoxy claims to be what its name means: the right dogma. In official circles the Orthodox grudgingly recognizes the existence of the other, more recent denominations of Judaism, i.e., Reform, Conservatism, and Reconstructionism. Orthodoxy posits that it is original Judaism, unchanged and unchangeable, and that since God gave the immutable Law on Sinai, we are still bound to follow it today as it came down to us.

This philosophy of Judaism does not consider that its claim

to be the original product cannot be defended. Between the time the Bible was begun and the time that the "Old Testament" was canonized, Judaism had already begun to change. The period of the prophets and, later, of the rabbis, further changed Judaism. In fact, modern Orthodoxy reflects the admixture of Talmudic and immediately post-Talmudic Judaism. Since the official Orthodox position is that prophecy came to an end with the last of the Biblical prophets, then nothing new could be added to Judaism with respect to theology from that time forth.

The result of that understanding is that modern Orthodoxy draws its approach to today from the writings of that medieval time, and interprets today's questions—including those of contemporary sexuality—in the light of the teachings of those times.

This methodology comes from a particular psychology and understanding of the contemporary universe, and in one sense provides the rationale by which Orthodoxy claims to have the right to dictate the manner in which one lives. The system works like this:

> Modern man grows up in a permissive family and community situation with little knowledge of the do's and dont's of behavior and little in the way of internal patterns of restraint built into his personality. This absence of an internal standard founded on an everpresent tradition, which in former times would be periodically reinforced by ritualistically and symbolically meaningful rites, is further perpetuated by the adolescent peer culture which takes on more significance than the family and the community as an arbiter of behavioral standards, and which compounds the individual's difficulties by offering an additional set of standards. While this may structure and define the world, thereby reducing anxiety, it does so in a way which not only may be in conflict with the larger society, but also acts to reduce individual self-reliance and responsibility, with all the consequences this has for problems of individual maturity and responsible behavior in the community. (Epstein, 1967, p. xv)

This perception of the contemporary world posits that our lives are out of control. Therefore, logically the solution to the problem is to find a technique of control, a strategy which will strengthen one's sense of mastery over inner needs and the demands of the environment. Orthodoxy presents its case as being time-tested and true because it has served well over the generations. The "bottom line" in such an approach is that the laws and regulations remain unchangeable; it is up to the individual to accept them and integrate them into his or her life. Thus, the option in an Orthodox existence is to observe the letter and the spirit of the law, with the expectation that an individual who does so will lead a fulfilling and meaningful existence.

That there are many Orthodox Jews who live thus is not the question. But at the same time it must be acknowledged that even within Orthodoxy observance of the law covers a wide spectrum. Certainly any observant (read: Orthodox) Jew will be more stringent in the interpretation of traditional Jewish laws and customs than a non-traditional Jew would be. But within the traditional community itself there are still disputes about how strictly one should follow certain laws. An example of the variations in practice or interpretation is found in determining the number of times in a given period that a husband and wife should have intercourse: the law states only that they must engage in intercourse. It is the later interpretations which suggest the following: if a man is of strong constitution and has profitable pursuits at home, the couple should perform their "marriage duty" nightly; laborers who live and are employed in one city should perform such duties once a week. Then the law expands by saying that, actually, if the laborers are employed in the city in which they live, then they should perform their duty twice a week, but if employed in another city, once a week is sufficient. Those who were away for extended periods of time were required to fulfill their duty at least once a year!

This example of a law (requiring intercourse), and the interpretation of that law (how many times, how often), is presented to demonstrate that even within Orthodoxy the apparent rigidity is just that: apparent. There is an inconsistency in the Orthodox approach to contemporary life. This becomes manifest when the Orthodox claim to have the way as set forth in the law, and then observe the law in a variety of ways, some of which clearly contradict one another.

Yet, for this potential confusion, Orthodoxy still is truer to the traditional practices as they have developed in Jewish history than any other denomination of Judaism. Orthodoxy is consistent in that it always begins from the premise that the legal ruling on an issue is the basis on which one makes decisions about something. Whatever the Talmud said about something in the past is the starting point for a discussion of an issue in the present. This is quite different from the approach of Reform (or liberal) Judaism, a discussion of which follows.

Modern Reform Jewish Practice

Reform Judaism had its beginnings in Germany in the middle of the last century. It was a response to the assimilation which was sweeping through the Jewish community, once the Jews began to leave the ghettos of Europe. While the movement was attacked bitterly by the Orthodox, both in its early years and even today, it has grown to be a very powerful force in the world Jewish community.

Its premise, with regard to human sexuality, is consonant with its approach to all other facets of human life and endeavor: respect the tradition, but not at the expense of asserting one's freedom to make life choices based on rational processes and ample information. Another way of phrasing this is to say that slavish adherence to ancient law is not necessarily the best way of fully experiencing one's Jewishness. A few examples of the differences between the Orthodox and Reform approaches to certain issues will clarify the point. First, with regard to divorce: Orthodoxy requires that a divorce clause be included in the mandatory marriage contract. Divorce is recognized as valid in Orthodoxy, but only under certain specific conditions, and even then, the husband has far broader rights to divorce than does the wife. Reform does not require a marriage contract, but recognizes the validity of a legal document in which a divorce clause might appear. Since Reform recognizes the full equality of women in all areas, then it must do so in the case of divorce as well. This means that a woman has the same rights to sue for divorce as a man has, on the same grounds.

Second, with respect to abortion: Orthodoxy is far more strict about when a woman may have an abortion. For the Orthodox the critical issue is the health of the mother; if the fetus is perceived as threatening the health or life of the mother, abortion is permitted. Reform expands this to include the mental health of the mother, and, recently, there has been some discussion of expanding the interpretations even further.

Third, with regard to homosexuality: Orthodoxy maintains a remarkably unflinching stand on this subject, claiming that as strict a construction of the Biblical position be adhered to as is permissible without the taking of a life. This seems to stem from the belief that homosexuality is a direct threat to the solidity and sanctity of the family as well as to the future of the generations of Jews yet unborn. There are those in the Orthodox community who suggest hating the "sin" but loving the "sinner," but this view is not universally shared even there. Until recently, almost all denominations of Judaism have followed this thinking. But within the last five years, the Reform movement has been making an effort to reevaluate its position on homosexuality, with the result that its major institutions have stated positions much less inimical than those of the Orthodox. For the Reform community the question is becoming less one of whether one is homosexual or not, and more one of whether one is prepared to cast one's lot fully with the Jewish community. It seems too early to tell if this signals a growing acceptance of homosexuality as a viable lifestyle within Reform, but indications are that such a move is taking shape.

Fourth, with respect to adultery: Orthodoxy is unflinching. The man is always the suspected offender, but both parties are to be punished. The offense is grave; the attitude toward it equally so. Reform looks no less harshly on the act or its perpetrator, but is less harsh with the punishment expected. Reform characteristically refers such things to civil authorities, since it claims no ultimate authority over its adherents, granting them relatively full religious autonomy within the life situation in which they find themselves.

Fifth, with regard to masturbation: Orthodoxy considers this an exceptionally grave sin, basing its approach on the (erroneous) assumption that spilling the sperm is equivalent to taking a life, and that one may become depleted of sperm and potentially be unable to fulfill the commandment to "be fruitful and multiply." This attitude reflects the philosophy of the family's ultimate importance. Since Reform Judaism has started to face the question of the "sanctity" of the nuclear family, it has also begun to question some of the corollary propositions which accompany that major premise. In other words, all of human sexuality has once again come under scrutiny in Reform Judaism, and, at this writing, masturbation is not perceived as an inherently evil act, threatening the future of Jews and Judaism. Reform understands human sexuality to be more than simply a vehicle for procreation; it sees it as a means of increasing emotional intimacy as well. In addition, responsible recreational sex, not used for recreation, is considered appropriate within Reform as well, preferably within the context of marriage. This attitude, then, allows for varieties of sexual expression not considered appropriate by Orthodoxy.

Reform and Orthodoxy represent the ends of a continuum in many respects, one of which is human sexuality. The two additional denominations of Judaism fall somewhere in between these two. These denominations, Conservative and Reconstructionist Judaism, are similar in many ways, especially in their being less stringent than the Orthodox and less liberal than Reform.

Conclusion

The overriding consideration of Judaism on the subject of human sexuality is that it be healthy and used for the good of humanity. For that reason, even when Orthodoxy regulates sexual conduct with laws and customs, it does so with the understanding that sexuality is potentially good, and that humanity stands to gain from the healthy expression of it. The finetuning of philosophies of sexuality within and among the Jewish denominations only serves once again to verify the quip with which this paper began: where there are two Jews, there will be three opinions. Fortunately, that seems to be all for the best, since all of the Jewish opinions affirm the basic goodness of human sexuality.

BIBLIOGRAPHY

Borowitz, Eugene B. *Choosing a Sex Ethic.* New York, Schocken Books, 1969.
Cohen, Seymour J. *The Holy Letter: A Study in Medieval Jewish Sexual Morality.* New York: KTAV Publishing, 1976.
Epstein, Louis M. *Sex Laws and Customs in Judaism.* New York: KTAV Publishing House, Inc., 1967.

Feldman, David M. *Birth Control in Jewish Law*. New York: New York University Press, 1968.

Gordis, Robert. *Sex and the Family in the Jewish Tradition*. New York: Burning Bush Press, 1967.

Lacks, Roslyn. *Women and Judaism: Myth, History and Struggle*. New York: Doubleday & Company, 1980.

Wouk, Herman. *This Is My God*. New York: Dell Publishing Co., Inc., 1964.

Chapter Three
ROMAN CATHOLIC VIEWS OF SEXUALITY

James H. Schulte, Ph.D.

The task of discussing Roman Catholic views of sexuality is hazardous. Should the approach be historical? If so, how complete must it be? Should it focus on the official position of the Church? A theological approach requires that one examine both aspects of the question. On the other hand, a more popular approach is possible. The polarization in the Church today might be an acceptable beginning. Or perhaps the views of the various groups who vie for attention in Roman Catholic circles might serve as an appropriate outline. For instance, one might consider the growing feminist perspective, the desires of the divorced and remarried Catholics, or the homosexual community's needs. Perhaps the concerns of the married Catholics who look for relief in the area of artificial contraceptions should be discussed. Nevertheless, since this essay is being directed to those concerned with sex therapy, a more fundamental consideration is necessary. Therefore, I shall attempt to discuss the Roman Catholic views of sexuality by exploring the question, "What are the moral convictions of Roman Catholics today, and why are they what they are?"

Until recently Roman Catholic views on sexuality were perceived (somewhat incorrectly) as being monolithic. Yet the proceedings of the recent 1980 Synod of Bishops in Rome illustrates that not all Catholics share identical views, even among members of the episcopacy. Whereas some of the assembled bishops clearly desired to reaffirm traditional church teachings, others among them seemed to be sensitive to the growing numbers of people in the church who did not share the convictions held by their church leaders. Consequently, this latter group of bishops requested a new, more positive theology of sexuality. The recognition that the monolithic perception of the recent past is no longer valid, if indeed it ever was, is perhaps the most important point to be made in this essay. In response to the first part of our question then, "What are the moral convictions of Roman Catholics?," we must respond that they are varied, covering a range of views —from a very conservative perspective to a very liberal one. It remains to be seen what effect the latest efforts of the world's Catholic Bishops and the official church in Rome will have on this diversity of opinion.

THREE VIEWS

For practical purposes, I would like to discuss three distinct divisions that I think are present among Roman Catholics today, three sets of "moral convictions," and the reasons that they are "what they are." The division is artificial and somewhat arbitrary, but it should serve to illustrate the range of positions within Roman Catholic thought, and therefore, to provide parameters for the therapists trying to understand the convictions of their clients.

The Older View

In describing the first group, I use the term "the older view" simply to designate the view that most observers of Roman Catholic views of sexuality are most familiar with. It is the classical stereotype perceived in certain sociological and psychological circles, as the typical Roman Catholic view. One could refer to this as the traditional view, or the conservative view, but such identifications are "loaded" with meaning not intended. Further, as I hope to show, the history of Catholic teaching presents a variety of views often overlooked. The moral convictions of this older view can be summarized as follows:

Chapter Three

Sexuality must be understood within the context of the generative purpose of sex. Sex is considered to be natural, a part of human makeup, intended to accomplish human generation. As such, it has a "natural" purpose or end, and this is then governed by the "natural law." This law is knowable through the use of reason; it is capable of being obeyed by the exercise of human will power, aided by God. Sexuality is a "lower power" in man, thus it must be supervised by the "higher powers" in man, the reason and the will. Sexual pleasure is an incentive to accomplish the purpose or end of sexual activity, generation, and from this flows the role of reason in directing the pleasure to its proper purpose. This, however, is difficult, because of human sinfulness and because of the strength of the pleasure involved. There remains the possibility of the sexual pleasure becoming "inordinate" pleasure which is then sinful. So the misdirection of sexual activity away from its proper end or purpose is also sinful.

One way to illustrate all of this is to consider an old concept. Since the purpose of sex is generation, the early church fathers turned to the example of animal generation for guidance as to what was natural to both animals and man. In that view, based upon an early and inadequate biology, the key to generation was the male semen, which was considered to be the sole source of human generation. The female was considered to be only the receptacle for that semen. In other words, the garden in which the seed was to grow. The purpose or end of semen naturally was offspring. Human offspring, however, required more than just generation; because of the dignity of human beings, they also required education. From this we could learn a great deal about what was appropriate in the area of moral convictions. Consider this diagram.

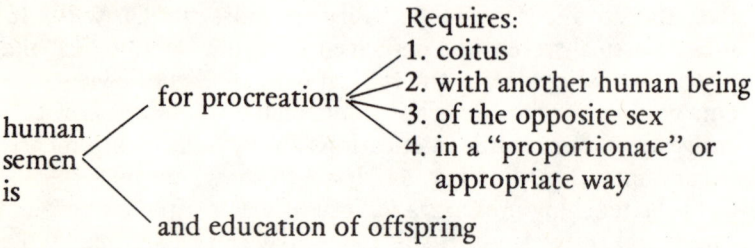

From this diagram it is possible to derive a number of moral convictions concerning sexual do's and dont's. Since the purpose of semen is procreation, and since procreation requires education, fornication is forbidden (as is adultery), for it does not insure adequate education of human offspring. Further, since procreation requires coitus, masturbation is forbidden. To do this is to waste the seed (the sole source of human generation). Since it requires human intercourse, bestiality is forbidden. Since procreation requires intercourse with the opposite sex, homosexuality is forbidden. And finally, since no procreation will take place if the procedure is inappropriate or lacks proper proportion, sodomy and onanism (birth control that is artificial) are forbidden. Indeed, each of these last four described activities is seen as unnatural, in that they are contrary to the natural order of things and the purpose of semen. Fornication and adultery on the other hand, along with incest and rape, do not violate the natural purpose of semen, but rather, err by denying the second purpose of semen. They are therefore, not unnatural, but unjust, as they deny the purpose of the education of offspring. This last bit of reasoning, while consistent with the scheme developed, has caused no end of difficulty for theologians and Catholic teachers. An incredulous faithful are more caught up in familiar concerns and therefore reject the theologians' order and logic. Finally, we should note that there has been a fear that the deviation from any one of the points in the diagram will lead to a breakdown of the entire system. Thus, for example, the fear of any change in an element such as birth control.

The strength of this system is that it is neat and well-ordered. It regulates systematically a variety of sexual activities; it appeals to a sense of order, and it is easy to apply. Once an activity has been clearly defined, it can be placed in its appropriate slot in the diagram. Then, the degree of sinfulness involved can be determined. Since most of these acts are unnatural, one need not worry about the myriad circumstances that tend to clutter the human condition. Being unnatural, the acts are always wrong, regardless of circumstances.

The weakness of this system is that it is too "act oriented" rather than person oriented; it is grounded upon an outdated understanding of biology and it fails to see sexuality as having more than a generative purpose for humans. Traces of this theory can be found in Church teaching going all the way back to St. Augustine (d. 430). He spoke of the goods of marriage as being children, fidelity and sacramental indissolubility. Likewise, in modern times, the 1918 Code of Canon Law, which has been extensively quoted in catechisms since that date, defined the purpose of marriage as being first, the procreation and education of children, and second, the mutual support of the couple (and the alleviation of "concupiscence" or the desire for sexual activity).

Until recently, most Catholics have been instructed in at least the practical implications of this moral system, and are, therefore, trained to be very suspect of any thought or action contrary to this way of thinking. As a result, many Catholics today still experience strong guilt feelings if they deviate from this line of reasoning. Specifically, they experience a marked degree of anxiety when they find their own behavior incompatible with these teachings. Concomitantly, individuals who share this older view of sexual activity may be very indignant about the demands of activist homosexuals, particularly when their own inclination is totally heterosexual. Theologian proponents of this older view would point out the illogic of this self-righteous position, but the system lends itself to this kind of convoluted thinking.

The obvious weaknesses of this older line of thinking have for centuries caused problems for some Catholic theologians. These problems have contributed to the development of other lines of thought.

The Newer View

In this section the choice of title is again somewhat arbitrary. What is here referred to is a Roman Catholic view of sexuality which has co-existed with the older view for a long time, but which is less known. If the older view is traditional, the newer view is modern. It has flourished more in recent times, although it has roots that go back for centuries. If the older view is conservative, the newer view is liberal because it allows more room for individual resolution of problems, and is more open to modern insights. Nevertheless, the liberal ideas are difficult to attain.

Unlike the older view, which tends to equate sexuality with genitality, the newer view emphasizes sexuality in the understanding of human personhood. This view of sexuality is grounded in a view of personhood that is less biological and more relational. It looks upon "natural law" as determinable, not so much from observing nature, but rather from a study of "the human person and his acts." It places less emphasis upon *what* a person is doing (act centered) and more emphasis upon *who* is doing it (personal) and *why* they are doing it (motivational). Greater emphasis is also placed on the role of human love in concert with moral convictions.

Traces of this newer approach are very old and very official in Catholic teaching. John Chrysostom, one of the early church fathers, wrote about human love. The sixth century penitentials (manuals for confessors) mitigated penances in matters sexual, depending upon the state in life and economic conditions of the penitents. (For example, a poor widow received a lesser penance for the same act than did an individual not so doubly afflicted.) In the twelfth century, Hugh of St. Victor spoke about the role of love in marriage. Among the other early and formidable theologians who contributed to the development of more personal considerations were: John Damascene (eighth century), Albert the Great (thirteenth century—and the teacher of St. Thomas Aquinas), Martin LeMaistre, and John Major (both fifteenth century). More recently, at the turn of the century, Dietrich von Hildebrand and Herbert Doms wrote about the meaning of marriage in the new vein. Perhaps equally important, official church teaching began to reflect the changing emphasis, culminating in the work of the Second Vatican Council, and the document *The Church in the Modern World* (1965). In this document, articles 48–52 develop a new theology of marriage which contrasts sharply with the traditional view. This theology demonstrates a new vision of sexuality. The dignity of the individual person and society in general is stressed, whereas the traditional emphasis is placed upon natural or unnatural acts. Marriage is seen as a community of love (within which offspring may—or may not—be generated and reared), rather than just a procreative contractual union. Illicit acts are not so much seen as contrary to natural ends of the institution of marriage. Rather they are selfish and against the character of human love. Social and economic changes in society are seen as factors in the understanding of marital problems. The input of sociology and psychology in theological and moral discussion is lauded. Childless families are accepted; love rather than procreation is seen as the motive for sexual activity. In sum, it is the moral goodness and dignity of human love (personal and relational), expressed in conjugal relations, that provides the new base for sexual morality. The dynamics of human growth and interpersonal integration are pivotal to our understanding of human sexual expression.

This newer way of thinking is abundantly evident in current Catholic documentation. Even the 1976 declaration of the Sacred Congregation for the Doctrine of the Faith, on *Certain Questions Concerning Sexual Ethics,* speaks of the fact that "it is from sex that the human person receives the characteristics which, on the biological, psychological and spiritual levels, make the person a man or a woman, and thereby largely condition his or her progress towards maturity and insertion into society." Although the document goes on to take a rather traditional approach to the particular questions dealt with (e.g., homosexuality, masturbation, etc.), the new direction of the opening remarks is quite clear.

In this newer approach, moral convictions regarding sexuality are derived from an understanding and appreciation of human dignity and personhood. Human activity must be judged by its contribution to or detraction from human growth and interpersonal integration. Individual acts have no meaning if separated from the person(s) involved or removed from their social context. Purely subjective morality is thus avoided by the role acknowledged to society, past and present, ecclesial and secular, in providing a context within which individuals act. Social and cultural guidelines must be respected, but not absolutized. Values must be striven for, but laws can change.

The strength of this newer view is that it is not as legalistic or as impersonal as the older view. It is relational and interpersonal, open to society and to scientific input. Its weakness is that it is less practical, lacks systematic development, and is subject to abuse. Many also feel it fails to give sufficient attention to human sinfulness. Surely, the uncontrolled quest for sexual gratification does result in massive human pain in our society today. It is these kinds of fears, along with the fear of departing from the older, more formalized and systematized scheme for sexual morality, that causes many in the

Church to restrain from accepting this newer approach.

For those Roman Catholics who have accepted this kind of thinking, the results can be tremendously freeing. They are able to live their lives in a more relaxed manner in the realm of sexual concerns. They are less threatened by others' behavior and are more tolerant of those who engage in sexual activity that deviates from the older norms. (This statement is not meant to imply that deviation from the older norms is necessarily to be desired, but only that tolerance is a healthy attitude in the realm of human sexual adjustment.) They tend to be at ease with their own sexuality, and are more self-directed in determining their own sexual conduct. The activist homosexual, referred to earlier, cannot be merely categorized as deviant and unnatural by followers of this newer system. Homosexuals must be dealt with as humans seeking personal and social growth.

The Middle View

A third group of Roman Catholics can be described, who I think fit in neither the older nor the newer category. This group is large; they are potentially the largest constituency. They are individuals who have been more or less exposed to the teachings of the older view and possibly have been exposed to the teachings of the newer view. Individuals representative of this middle viewpoint usually have been exposed to both views. They now have doubts about their earlier education. For practical purposes they have rejected it—at least as it applied to some aspects of their personal life. Influenced as much by the mores of the day as the concerns of theological debate, they have arrived at a point where they operate generally upon their own conscience or their own perception of what they should do in the area of sexual ethics.

An interesting aspect of these individuals is that they often are vigorous defenders of the traditional views as far as the current public teaching of the Church is concerned. They fail or are unwilling to see that their own behavior contradicts that teaching.

This group is large, as witnessed by the statistics concerning the number of Catholics who have rejected the church's older teaching on birth control, and the numbers who still frequent the sacraments. In his address to the world Synod of Bishops, Archbishop John Quinn spoke of the 71% of American Catholic women who reject the church's position on birth control. Others have claimed even higher percentages.

Many of these individuals typify a pattern of development on matters of human sexuality. Collectively or individually they found an area where the older teaching of the church no longer was compatible with their personal behavior. They felt that the teaching no longer was compelling because of circumstances they were experiencing. Perhaps the problem was artificial birth control. Their experience of marriage suggested that there was a lot more to marital life than procreation. Perhaps they sought out a priest who could concur with their emerging views. Stories of such shopping expeditions are legion. At one time, the news of such a counselor's existence was considered highly-privileged information. Perhaps they became comfortable with their new approach to a nagging problem, only to learn that the church did not approve of the advice they had been given. By that time they were sufficiently comfortable with their approach to be unwilling to change, with or without the advice of a confessor. Yet, these individuals often discover that their past training can cause a degree of anxiety in their new way of living. Or they may find that having rejected one area of church teaching, other areas are now equally easily dismissed. This may lead to deviations they are not ready to be comfortable with. Lacking the fortification of a system of values for decision making, this may lead to further experiments. Conditions such as this can, it seems to me, lead to a high degree of anxiety; this in turn, can lead directly to sexual disfunctioning, born of feelings of guilt.

The strength of this approach to Catholic sexual ethics is that it allows for the greatest degree of autonomy and personal freedom. It is highly adaptable to the countless human situations proper to our age.

The weakness of this system lies in its very unstructured and eclectic strength—it is totally free. Cast against the usual Catholic educational background, this can in turn lead to excessive guilt. As such, this system can become insensitive to the needs of others, and is therefore often destructive of human interpersonal relationships. Like the newer approach previously described, this method often fails to sufficiently allow for human sinfulness—to destroy self or others, to do real harm. Lacking a systematic approach, it may fail to adequately fortify the individual who needs to make a well thought out and consistent ethical decision.

In other words, Catholics engaged in this third approach in the area of sexuality, may find it to be a dangerous procedure. The experience can be very freeing, and can serve to meet short term needs to resolve pressing problems. There exists, however, the very real danger of finding that the solution lacks sufficient depth. Old fears reemerge in the vacuum that can result when a previously held system of values is rejected and replaced with solutions to particular problems rather than to a system. Further, there is a danger that the new freedom may be abused and that the immediate good achieved gives way to long-range bad consequences. Finally, tolerance with one's own value system can carry with it an intolerance for all other value systems. Deviant behavior can become synonymous with any behavior that deviates from one's own!

THE CATHOLIC PROBLEM

Three distinct views of human sexual values that are dominant among members of the Roman Catholic community today in the United States have been presented. That they are not harmonious is, I think, clear. For many who subscribe to the older tradition, the very existence of the other two viewpoints is a source of anger and frustration. These individuals would view such deviation as an indication of heresy. (It is not, given the history of the development of Catholic moral teaching in this and a variety of other areas.) Many would also see these other views as divisive, and as a source of moral decline in the Church. (It need not be.) Many bishops, priests and theologians do not share these attitudes. They may not support the newer or middle view, because they see in both of them weaknesses they cannot tolerate, and feel that such diversity cannot be tolerated because of the effects upon the faithful. In other words, they may be attracted to a more personal approach to matters of sexual concern, but feel that the latter systems are not sufficiently well-grounded to be made compatible with the older, safer and more familiar approach.

Conversely, those who support the newer approach are at times tolerant of the older position and its supporters. Many of them would also admit that the danger is present in the newer approach to leave too much to individual judgment, given the tendency for people to be too forgiving of their own behavior. They have a degree of difficulty in denying the charge that the new system fails to allow sufficiently for human sin. Supporters of the newer approach are also often too quick to criticize the official church statements concerning sexuality, statements which must take into consideration the needs of many Catholics not yet sufficiently mature or educated in the newer approach, and those in a variety of nations not even aware of the existence of a different system.

Catholics who fall into the third category present the biggest problem to those in both of the other two groups. Individuals who have rejected the older system without becoming aware of the newer, are often disinterested in either system and may eventually reject the very right of any religious body to have a distinctive position on matters of morality.

The request of the American Bishops at the 1980 Synod of Bishops for a long range study in the area of sexuality by both church leaders and scholars would seem to be a move in the direction of resolving the problems suggested above.

For the sexual therapist, the problem appears to be one of determining just who is being dealt with when the therapist has a "Catholic client." Is the individual one whose moral convictions are born of a belief in the older approach to sexual ethics? But what if the client is coming from the newer perspective? Surely, a totally different approach would be called for. And if the client is coming out of the third or middle approach? Obviously this could include a great variety of individual viewpoints. Is this actually a "Catholic" view of sexuality at all? Yet large numbers of Catholics today hold such views, and must be dealt with. Perhaps the therapist must recognize members of this group for what they are. They are like travelers who have left a distinctive approach (some would say an extreme one) and are on their way to another. They have perhaps not yet arrived at that new one, but they are definitely not where they were before. I would think that they present a particular problem for the counselor.

CONCLUSION

This discussion of Roman Catholic views of sexuality has thus far offered three distinct views that can be currently identified in the Catholic community. Each has a different set of convictions; each derives its impetus from different factors in the Catholic/Christian tradition. The older and newer views both claim to influence Catholic value systems and Catholic moral teaching. Almost all of the individuals described still characterize themselves as "Catholic"; studies indicate that a high percentage of each group still receive the sacraments of the church. Yet the three systems remain difficult, if not impossible to harmonize.

I think one question remains that may hold the key for the future. Why has this state of disarray in Catholic thinking developed at this particular moment in history? The answer I think lies both within our society in general and within the church in particular. On the part of society, there are tremendous forces at work to recognize the rights of individual persons. Since the holocaust of World War II, an almost universal conviction to uphold individual dignity and right has developed. This has resulted in a variety of phenomena, some positive and some negative. Obviously it has contributed to additional wars as peoples have struggled to achieve their personal and national rights. Also it has motivated great numbers of previously suppressed peoples within individual nations to seek liberation from any form of suppression and discrimination. One can think of equal rights efforts of the blacks, the homosexual community, and most recently, the women of this country. The so-called sexual revolution is at least in part inspired by this desire and experience—Catholics are not immune from such cultural pressures.

On the part of the church, the events leading up to, including and following the second Vatican Council, are a testimony to the same phenomenon on an individual denominational level. That council is a remarkable testimony to the vision of its participants in recognizing the signs of the times and responding to them. That such an event in a major religious community should result in a variety of insights as to where its pronouncements should logically lead can hardly be surprising. Nowhere is this more evident than in the area of sexual ethics.

The council indicates that sexuality must be viewed in a new way, from a more personal and relational perspective. What this means in practice, what this means for individual moral convictions, was not spelled out. Some feel the framework of a new articulation must remain within the older framework. Other feel a newer framework is required, and these perspectives provide such. Still others are content to agree that it must be viewed in a new way and are happy to provide their own way as adequate for themselves. Thus, three views.

Currently, those who would maintain the older view are for the most part, fighting a holding action. They are little interested in dialogue with anyone who disagrees with them, closed to any innovation in moral teaching. Those who would build a new system of sexual ethics are having little success in developing a dialogue with those who hold the older view. The free spirits, liberated from the older approach and disinterested in the newer, seem content at present, content to go it alone. Perhaps only time will lead to a meeting of minds, but there seems little likelihood of a return to the former pre-Vatican II state of affairs.

The sexual therapist must then adjust to a varied menu of Catholic clientele in his/her therapy. Catholics are hardly immune from sexual disfunctioning, and sooner or later, representative numbers from each of the three approaches are likely to seek counseling. Their divergent moral convictions and the rationale behind them must be recognized and dealt with by the prudent counselor, who is concerned with the question "What are the moral convictions of Roman Catholics today, and why are they what they are?"

The varied state of Catholic thought discussed above is a source of anxiety for many Catholics. This anxiety is not shared by me. The human condition is a dynamic and evolving condition. Growth in the area of sexuality and in the moral convictions that attend this subject is a necessary ingredient in the dynamism that is life. Sexual disfunction is a symptom of a lack of wellness, and its correction involves a return to life-giving dynamics in personal and interpersonal relationships. From that perspective, the present condition is promising, and as a commentator on the moral scene, I welcome the opportunity to be a contributor to sexual wellness. In that quest, the sexual therapist should be a potent force for good.

BIBLIOGRAPHY

Dedek, John. *Contemporary Sexual Morality.* New York: Sheed and Ward, 1971.

Abbott, Walter, ed. *The Documents of Vatican II.* New York: Guild, 1966.

Greeley, Andrew; McCreedy, William; and McCourt, Kathleen. *Catholic Schools in a Declining Church.* Kansas City: Sheed and Ward, 1975.

Hoyt, R. G., ed. *The Birth Control Debate.* Kansas City: National Catholic Reporter, 1978.

Joannes, R. V., ed. *The Bitter Pill.* Philadelphia: Pilgrim Press, 1970.

Keane, Phillip S. *Sexual Morality.* New York: Paulist Press, 1977.

Kosnik, A.; Carroll, W.; Cunningham, A.; Modras R.; and Schulte, J. *Human Sexuality: New Directions in American Catholic Thought.* A study commissioned by the Catholic Theological Society of America. New York: Paulist Press, 1977.

Chapter Four
PROTESTANT VIEWS OF SEXUALITY

Letha Scanzoni, B.A.

Beginning with the Reformation, Protestants have commented about human sexuality. Martin Luther, for example, took issue with church teachings which exalted celibacy and downgraded marriage. To Luther, sexual desire was natural and necessary, a mysterious power designed and implanted in human beings by God. He also disagreed with the notion of a soul-body split which associated the body with sin, sex with shame, and which saw redemption in self-denial (Feucht et al., 1961, pp. 75-78).

Luther's Realism

Luther admitted his sexual temptations during celibacy. He once advised a friend to marry because of the friend's strong sex drive, which Luther saw as indicating a *need* to be married. As Luther interpreted Scripture, marriage was the means designed by God to satisfy sexual urges. Many of the church's teachings on sexuality struck Luther as being unrealistic—not only teachings on compulsory vows of celibacy for priests, nuns, and monks, but also certain forms of penance required at that time. For example, a wife and husband might be told to sleep together, yet abstain from all sexual contact. "They put dry wood on a fire and say, 'Don't burn!'" exploded Luther.

"Luther saw an urgency and a compulsion in sex that simply could not be denied in normal persons," a group of Lutheran scholars point out. "This is why he expressed himself so freely in matters of sex." They add that his realism and plain speech about sexual matters has offended some persons, while being welcomed by others (Feucht et al., 1961, p. 85).

Yet, Luther was a product of his times; many of his views lack certain positive ideas and ideals about sex and marriage widely held among Protestants today. It should be remembered, however, that Luther wrote over many years; some of his views on sexuality and marriage changed over time. Luther, like most other Reformers, emphasized that a major purpose of marriage was to "avoid fornication." He also saw marriage as providing human beings with the wonderful opportunity to have and rear children. Luther viewed marriage as a setting in which the highest type of neighbor-love could be expressed (Feucht et al., 1961, pp. 81–83).

Calvin's Views

John Calvin, another leader of the Protestant Reformation, used an "illness" analogy, as Luther had also done in his early writings. Calvin spoke of strong sexual desire as an "infirmity" requiring God's remedy—marriage. "The conjugal relation was ordained as a necessary means of preventing us from giving way to unbridled lust," he wrote. "Let us beware, therefore, of yielding to indulgence, seeing we are assured that the curse of God lies on every man and woman cohabiting without marriage" (*Institutes,* Book II, Chap. VIII, Sec. 41).

Even *within* marriage, Calvin called for restraint. He instructed both husbands and wives "not to do anything unbecoming the dignity and temperance of married life." In Calvin's thinking, "though honourable wedlock veils the turpitude of incontinence, it does not follow that it ought forthwith to become a stimulus to it." And in a statement foreshadowing Pope John Paul II's 1980 warning that husbands might commit adultery in their hearts by looking with excessive desire at their wives, the sixteenth century Calvin referred to Ambrose, who "described the man who shows no modesty of comeliness in conjugal intercourse as committing adultery with his wife" (*Institutes,* Book II, Chap. VIII, Sec. 44).

A certain ambivalence about sexuality is contained in the

writings of the Reformers. On the one hand, they considered it to be a holy and honorable creation of God; on the other hand, they worried about "too much" sexual desire. Because sin had entered the world, "lust" was like a fire that might get out of control. "The immoderate degree with which persons burn is a fault arising from the corruption of nature," wrote Calvin in his commentary on Corinthians (quoted in Feucht et al., p. 107). "But," he continued, "in the case of believers, marriage is a veil by which the fault is covered over so that it no longer appears in the sight of God."

Protestant Thinking Today

Moving from the Reformation to Protestantism today, I want first, to stress a point made by Jean Caffey Lyles in an editorial in the *Christian Century* (October 29, 1980, p. 1027). Lyles emphasizes that U.S. Christians can no longer be neatly divided into two major alignments: Catholic and Protestant. Three major alignments now exist: Catholic, mainline Protestant, and evangelical. Evangelicals have been in the news and have recently become more politically active. Sexologists need to understand evangelical thinking on sexuality—especially if we are to effectively promote and carry out school and community sex education programs and provide help for clients from conservative Christian backgrounds who request counseling.

Evangelical Protestantism

In the United States, the word *evangelical* applies to those Christians who emphasize a personal faith commitment to Jesus Christ—an experience also termed: "born again," "saved," "redeemed," "converted," or "accepting Christ as personal Saviour." They also are usually concerned about spreading "the good news of salvation" or evangelizing. (The word *evangel* derives from a Greek word meaning "bearer of good news.") Evangelicals commonly emphasize the authority of Scripture in doctrine and daily life (Quebedeaux, 1974, 1978; Bloesch, 1978).

Evangelicalism has its historic roots in the Great American Religious Awakening and revivals of the eighteenth and nineteenth centuries. The fundamentalist/modernist controversy surfaced in the late nineteenth and early twentieth centuries.

Now I realize that both suggestiveness and exhaustion are fairly common sexual experiences. I will try to opt for the former and simply be suggestive (not exhaustive) on each of these themes! (Nelson, 1978).

1. *I would like to see us move from theologies of or about human sexuality to sexual theologies.* (Thus, a more accurate title for this whole presentation would be "Toward a Sexual Theology.")

Carl Jung once commented that when people brought religious questions to him they always turned out to be sexual questions; when they brought sexual questions they were really religious questions. He was aware that the direction of traffic is two-way and not one-way. But the vast majority of religious or theological books, articles, statements and declarations on sexuality over the centuries have assumed a one-way question: namely, what does theology (or the Bible or the tradition) say about human sexuality. I propose that we take a clue from those who today are writing that Black Theology, Feminist Theology, and Third World Liberation Theology reflect human experience (in those instances, the experience of oppression) and afford extraordinarily important insights into the meanings of religious faith itself.

Thus, my concern is two-way. It is dialogical, not monological. In addition to the question "What do our religious traditions say about human sexuality?" (still a very important question), I want also and at the same time to press the question "What does our experience as sexual human beings say about the ways we experience God, about the ways we interpret our religious traditions, and about the ways we attempt to live out the meanings of our faiths?" And this leads directly to my second proposition.

2. *I would like us to move from seeing sexuality as incidental to our experience of God to seeing it utterly essential to that experience.* (At this point, let me be clear that I am speaking from a Christian viewpoint, specifically a liberal Protestant viewpoint, but I believe that each of these propositions is relevant to the Jewish faith as well.)

How, then, is God experienced in human life? How does God make the divine presence, power, and purpose known and real in the lives of people? Christian faith makes that bold, indeed startling, claim that the most decisive experience of God occurs not in ideas, doctrine, creed, mystical otherworldly experience—but in *flesh*. Hence, the opening words of the Gospel according to John:

> In the beginning was the Word, and the Word was with God, and the Word was God . . . And all things were made through the Word, and without the Word was not anything made that was made . . . . And the Word became flesh and dwelt among us, full of grace and truth.

Here, then, is a religion of incarnation. In-carne, as in chili con carne—with meat! Enfleshment. The embodiment of God.

Christians confess that they have seen God most decisively, with greatest clarity and focus, in and through one human being, Jesus the Christ. Yet it is a profound theological error, I believe, to limit the incarnation to that historic figure. In so doing we both deny his genuine humanity and treat him as an exception to the general human condition—an anomaly. Furthermore, we close ourselves off from the central claim of an incarnationalist faith—that God continues to be most decisively experienced in the fleshly, embodied touching of human life with human life.

Word becoming flesh—this is communication, this is communion. The mystery of human sexuality is thus, the mystery of our need to reach out to embrace others physically, emotionally, spiritually. Our sexuality expresses God's intention that we find our authentic humanness not in isolation but in relationship. Our sexuality is God's way of inviting us to become "body-words of love," for our sexuality is both the physiological and psychological grounding of our capacity to love. And that applies to human-divine relationship as well as to the human to human.

3. *I would like to see us move from viewing sexual sin as wrong sexual acts to understanding sexual sin as alienation from our divinely-intended sexuality.* Now that is another fundamental shift in general understanding. If we were to take a poll of persons who counted themselves in any way religious and for whom the term "sin" had some meaning, and if we were to task them, "What is sexual sin?," the vast majority of responses would be predictable. Sexual sin, they would say, has to do with being too sexual or with certain types of acts—sex with the wrong person, or some kind of unnatural or harmful sex act. Now I am not dismissing such answers as necessarily

This controversy was focused on sharp differences of opinion regarding Biblical inerrancy and modern Biblical scholarship, with its critical methodology. The challenge to Biblical writings by scientific theory and research fueled this controversy. The Social Gospel Movement urged Christians to be socially and politically involved, thus adding to this struggle among Christians. Those who were committed to the inerrancy of the scriptures called for a return to the "fundamentals of the faith" and thus fundamentalism was born (Quebedeaux, 1978; Dayton 1977). Many left the mainline Protestant churches to form their own churches, schools, periodicals, para-church ministries, missionary societies, and a loosely-knit separate evangelical subculture based in large part around a particular approach to the Bible (Sheppard, 1977). Evangelicals have also been influenced by Puritanism (with its stress on obedience to the law of God) and Pietism (a movement that emphasized holy living and the avoidance of "worldly pleasures").

Evangelicals are not a monolithic group. Especially today! There are far-right *fundamentalists* who are extremely legalistic in personal conduct matters and reactionary on social issues. Conversely, left-wing or "radical" evangelicals, who are concerned with social justice and who are active in a variety of causes, are welcomed by the Protestant mainstream. In between, the continuum shows great diversity. Evangelicals have in common their emphasis on knowing Christ through a personal faith commitment. Beyond that, they disagree intensely among themselves about Biblical inspiration, authority, and interpretation—particularly as it pertains to the role of women, homosexuality, and other contemporary concerns (Johnston, 1979).

Nor are evangelicals easily distinguished or separated from other Protestants. Large numbers of evangelicals, including extremely conservative ones, remain in mainline denominations. Recently, they have influenced denominational debates on homosexuality and other issues related to human sexuality.

Most evangelicals agree—or at least acknowledge that sex is not something evil, but is a good gift of God. Most also believe that God has provided guidelines in Scripture for the use and expression of human sexuality, but warns about its abuse. In evangelical thought, the appropriate and ideal place for full sexual expression is marriage. Evangelicals tend to believe that

Biblical norms do not support premarital sex (the usual evangelical interpretation of Biblical warnings against fornication) nor extramarital sex (adultery).

There are a variety of "evangelical views" on such controversial issues as homosexuality or abortion. Traditionally, most evangelicals have believed that "homosexuality is sin." Recently, however, many have begun making a distinction between homosexual *orientation* (not sinful because unchosen) and homosexual *behavior* (sinful because such acts are viewed as violating biblical norms). Many evangelicals support gay civil rights. Although fundamentalists on the far right send out mailings and lead crusades that play upon homophobia and hostility toward gays, many other evangelicals care about homosexual personhood and speak about love and justice toward gay people. An emerging minority accept that homosexual love within a covenantal partnership may be analogous to heterosexual marriage; thus, it is acceptable in God's sight. (See Scanzoni and Mollenkott, 1978; the literature of Evangelicals Concerned; and the special June, 1978 issue of *The Other Side*.)

There are pro-life evangelicals on both ends of the spectrum. On the right, are those whose activities in the anti-abortion movement are also associated with support for militarism, capital punishment, curtailing aid to the poor, and opposition to the Equal Rights Amendment. At the other end of the spectrum, some evangelicals feel that an anti-abortion stance is the only consistent position open to them as pacifists. They are against nuclear weaponry, nuclear power, capital punishment, are concerned for the poor, committed to social justice, and identify themselves as feminists (see November, 1980 issue of *Sojourners*). At the same time, a significant number of evangelicals identify themselves as pro-*choice* —or at least take the position that the abortion issue is complex and must be approached on an individual, situational basis. (See J. Scanzoni, 1969; Gardner, 1972; and the special June, 1980 issue of *The Other Side*.)

Mainstream Protestantism

We will now move from evangelicalism to a consideration of mainstream Protestantism. Most mainline Protestant bodies are members of the National Council of Churches (NCC).

Statements on human sexuality made by divisions of the NCC, its representatives, member denominations, and mainline theologians, indicate an openness to the social and behavioral sciences and a desire to wrestle with profound theological questions about meaning and purpose—instead of simply focusing on outward sexual behavior (for example, Nelson, 1978). The emphasis is on guidelines for helping persons make moral decisions for themselves in the light of their Christian faith and with encouragement from the community of faith.

Typical of mainstream pronouncements on human sexuality are these excerpts from a 1976 "Resolution on the Family" published by the General Conference of the United Methodist Church:

> The Christian position is that God's creative and redemptive love is the basis on which all human relationships should be established. God's covenant with Israel and the event of Jesus Christ provide the model for those relationships.... In the strength of God's faithfulness to this covenant, we are called and enabled to live faithfully in human community. Significant ways of doing this include such expressions of our sexuality as establishing a marriage relationship and creating a family unit.
>
> Sexuality is a good gift from God and is a fundamental means of realizing the wholeness of life through its interrelationships. This gift includes all that it means to be male and female and is not limited to coital behavior. All expressions of human sexuality affect the emergence and development of the full worth of persons and should reflect a concern for personal integrity, faithfulness in relationships, and equality of women and men. (p. 2)

Theologian Robert McAfee Brown describes the "spirit of Protestantism" as "an openness to the judging and renewing activity of the living God made known in Jesus Christ." This includes a willingness "to submit to the corrective activity of God" and "a willingness to live at risk, not only because the claim to human security is a denial of God, but because when human securities have been destroyed, God can enter in" (Brown, 1965, p. 40).

Thus, mainstream theologians, Biblical scholars, and ethicists are likelier than many evangelicals to rethink matters of sexuality. Some mainline Protestants admit to having changed and even reversed their earlier conventional views (Pittenger, 1970, pp. 9–10). Some have concluded that "there is no biblical sex ethic" (Wink, 1979, p. 1085). In asserting that "the Bible has no sexual ethic," professor Walter Wink says, "The Bible knows only a love ethic, which is constantly being brought to bear on whatever sexual mores are dominant in any given country, or culture, or period."

Another professor and New Testament scholar, Victor Paul Furnish, cautions against treating the Bible—and specifically the moral teachings of Paul—as a "sacred cow" or contrarily, a "white elephant." The sacred-cow view assumes that the ethical teachings of Paul are binding for all times and for all persons, without consideration of cultural context. They are regarded as God's commandments; "if we are uncomfortable with, for example, the teaching in Paul's letters about slavery or hairstyles or subjection to earthly rulers, that is *our* problem, not the Bible's" (Furnish, 1979, p. 14). But equally to be avoided, says Furnish, is the white-elephant view which rejects Paul's moral teachings as though obsolete. To the contrary, readers are urged to understand the context in which the Apostle was writing, look for basic principles, and to see Paul's concern that "faith be enacted in love" (pp. 18–28). Furnish also contends that persons who treat the Bible as a sacred cow run the risk of "turning it into a white elephant" because they will find it simply doesn't treat all the urgent, specific concerns of the modern world (pp. 27–28).

The openness to new insight that Brown spoke of earlier in describing the spirit of Protestantism is evident in a statement from the United Presbyterian Church, U.S.A. as it deliberated with whether or not to ordain a homosexual person to the ministry. A committee report contained this statement:

> Because God continues to reveal more of himself and his will in each succeeding age, we do not believe that a position taken in any one period sets forth the final understanding of his Word to the Church. We know that there is always more light to break forth from the Bible through the work of the Holy Spirit. (Addition to the Report of the Assembly Committee on Bills and Overtures to the 188th Assembly, May 24, 1976. Mimeographed)

A special "Task Force to Study Homosexuality" was appointed to issue a report two years later for the 190th General Assembly. The majority report of the Task Force allowed for the possibility of ordaining qualified homosexual persons.

Conservative evangelicals, however, issued a minority report warning of the danger of following cultural trends and fallible human reason. "We have been charged to seek 'new light from God's Word,' not 'new light' contrary to God's Word" (Blue Book I, p. D-191).

In the end, the General Assembly adopted a report which in part read: "Our present understanding of God's will precludes the ordination of persons who do not repent of homosexual practice." The wording, "our present understanding," left open the possibility that the church might eventually change its mind (Lyles, 1978a, p. 603). That option was referred to in a moving speech by Paul S. Wright, an 83-year-old former moderator. "If we have spoken finalities here," said Wright, "then we have slammed the door on the winds of the Holy Spirit. We're more comfortable if the door is shut and we're not in a draft. But I trust the judgment of the Assembly. I don't think this action closes the door. There may be further light to come" (quoted in Lyles, 1978b, p. 638).

Resistance to Change and the "Politics of Life-style Concern"

Keeping the door shut against the winds of change and keeping the draperies drawn to make sure new light doesn't get through appeals to many persons. They want the security of settled answers. Many such persons are drawn to *conservative* Protestantism because it promises to provide those settled answers directly from God in the words of Scripture. This is a major reason for the appeal of the New Right movement within the evangelical wing.

"The Bible may be an antiquated book to many, but for the believer it is actually God speaking," declared Anita Bryant as she explained her efforts to have Dade County's gay rights ordinance repealed. "God says there are some things that are evil and some things that are good. That's simple enough for even a child to understand" (Bryant, 1977, p. 37). She later said that children are immature, however; thus they are unable to sort things out and make wise choices. In particular, according to Bryant, children need to be protected from homosexuality.

When groups holding strongly to a particular world view feel that they are threatened by those espousing other values, belief systems, and life-styles, they often mobilize their forces to engage in public resistance. They insist that *their* way is the *right* way. Sociologists of social movements refer to such struggles as "status politics" or "politics of life style concern" (Gusfield, 1963; Zurcher and Kirkpatrick, 1976; Page and Clelland, 1978). These "symbolic crusades" often focus on some issue that is seen as a threat to the family. Some examples are: sex roles, abortion, homosexuality, sex education in the schools, erotica, and the Equal Rights Amendment.

Groups that want to gain or regain dominance for their world view understand the necessity of influencing the "construction of reality" that verifies and buttresses that world view. In the words of Peter Berger and Thomas Luckmann, specialists in the sociology of knowledge, "The appearance of an alternative symbolic universe poses a threat because its very existence demonstrates empirically that one's own universe is less than inevitable" (Berger and Luckmann, 1967, p. 108). Organizers of religiously-based right-wing political movements thus want their way of life acknowledged by the passing of laws that support their values (or the repeal of ordinances that don't support their values). The socialization of children is considered especially important. Fundamentalist political activists often seek to gain influence and control, wherever possible, over such socialization agents as the media and the public schools. They especially want to keep children away from ideas associated with evolution, humanism, cultural pluralism, and moral relativism—the latter having provoked fears over sex education programs in public schools.

The idea of raising questions, thinking for oneself, and making choices is frightening to some persons (Fromm, 1941). Ambiguities and complexities are hard for them to tolerate; they want settled answers and simplistic solutions. The feeling was perhaps best summarized by a parent during a volatile textbook controversy in the Kanawha County, West Virginia school district in 1974. Frightened and angry over the ideas children were being exposed to, the parent exclaimed, "It's an insidious attempt to replace our periods with their question marks" (quoted in Page and Clelland, p, 276).

Changing Attitudes

Yet, life itself has a way of changing periods into question marks. The once self-assured Anita Bryant quoted earlier sounded quite different from the Anita Bryant of 1980 who says, "The answers don't seem quite so simple now" and who calls for attitudes of love, understanding, and "live and let live" toward gays; she now sees "valid reasons why militant feminists are doing what they're doing." Bryant reports that she "experienced a form of male chauvinism among Christians that was devastating" and has "about given up on the fundamentalists, who have become so legalistic and letter-bound to the Bible" (interview with Bryant by Jahr, 1980). Contributing to the change in Bryant's thinking was her own suffering in a marriage that she says almost destroyed her. This led her to violate fundamentalist norms by divorcing her husband without having "biblical grounds" (according to fundamentalist interpretation of Scripture).

Human experience often leads to theological rethinking. People find the rigid rules they've been taught are not always practical; the inflexible standards don't always meet human needs; the high ideals don't allow for human frailties; the unbending principles may intensify human pain without providing relief or escape. Human experience may therefore inspire religious leaders to reexamine Scripture, church tradition, theology, and insights from the behavioral sciences.

Most Protestant views of sexuality are in the ferment of biblical reinterpretation, theological reformulation, and changing attitudes. Although examples of such openness to change are more likely to be found among mainline bodies than within evangelical groups, a considerable amount of rethinking is also occuring among evangelicals—on such issues as abortion and homosexuality. This may be seen in some other areas as well (see Smedes, 1976).

Where rethinking is taking place, the movement is not a devil-may-care attitude in which "anything goes." On the contrary, the changes underscore a basic concern for the needs and feelings of persons instead of a slavish devotion to rigid principle. Principles need not be ignored, but must be flexible. The welfare of individual human beings is of prime consideration. For example, Protestants (even conservative ones) are much more tolerant or accepting of divorce than they once were (O'Neill, 1967). In principle, divorce is still considered wrong at worst or "less than God's ideal" at best. But to insist that persons remain trapped in a miserable marriage or that they may never remarry in the event of a divorce is considered incompassionate (Small, 1975).

Contraception is another area in which Protestants have shown change. Before the 1930s, Protestant leaders pronounced "the limitation of birth by artificial means both anti-social and anti-Christian," "pagan," "a menace to the family," "demoralizing to character and hostile to national welfare." "If this thing is going on, let it go on, but why should we endorse it?" said one bishop of the Episcopal Church, reflecting the views of those who felt churches should simply ignore the matter. Others, however, pointed out that millions of the laity were already using contraceptives and said it was about time the church recognized that fact and provided some guidance. Historian David Kennedy writes:

> Liberal theology, with its acceptance of science and its interpretation of lay experience as one manifestation of the divine plan, joined with a romantic view of the spiritual fruits of sexuality to provide a framework within which Protestant theologians could find moral justification for contraception.... The nineteenth century had regarded sexuality as a destructive force threatening the social order. Nothing more dramatically illustrated the obsolescence of that view by the 1930s than the liberal Protestant's understanding of sex as an instrumentality for the preservation of marriage. (Kennedy, 1970, p. 170)

Today, with few exceptions, conservative evangelical thinking reflects a similar viewpoint. The motives and methods of contraception are left up to the conscience of the individual couple, as is the decision about the *number* of children to have —although some conservative writers believe that it is displeasing to God to decide not to have any children at all (LaHaye and LaHaye, 1976).

Masturbation is a third area in which changing attitudes show up in Protestant writings. When Presbyterian minister Charlie Shedd wrote a book for teenagers in 1968 entitled *The Stork Is Dead,* he included a chapter called "Masturbation —Gift of God." Hate mail poured in—which didn't surprise him nor his publisher. Shedd, persuaded he was right, did not back down from his position. Eventually many of his most outspoken critics had a change of mind and began inviting him to speak to their groups; his book continues to be popular in both evangelical and mainline circles. Similarly, the editors of *Campus Life,* a publication of the evangelical youth organization, Youth for Christ, were surprised to find a panel of evangelical leaders agreeing on a positive view of masturbation in a 1972 telephone opinion survey (Landrum, 1972). On the other hand, when I took a positive approach to the topic of masturbation in a question and answer column for a 1978 issue of *The Other Side,* a leading periodical of the left-wing, radical, or progressive movement in evangelicalism, angry letters and threats to cancel subscriptions poured in! Neither I nor the editors expected this—especially since I received only positive response to a section on masturbation in my 1973 sex education book, *Sex Is a Parent Affair.* Evidently, in spite of overall changing attitudes (especially among younger people and among women), some evangelicals don't yet feel comfortable about masturbation.

Grappling with New Issues

Many parents and religious leaders are finally beginning to recognize the tremendous challenges to rethink human sexuality that confront us today. Many people aren't quite sure how to handle those challenges. In speaking to Protestant youth groups, I have heard adolescents frequently say that they wish adults wouldn't treat sex secretly or as something "dirty" and taboo. Children would like to talk with their parents about the questions on their minds, but don't feel they can. High school and college men and women often analyze issues from a perspective their parents never had. The younger generation may have friends who are homosexual and other friends who are living together. They may be sexually experienced themselves. The old answers and warnings given by their parents don't quite fit their experiences; yet they're seeking moral guidelines.

Defining Marriage (or The Cohabitation Question)

Most Protestants are asking questions about marriage. Why are many young persons rejecting marriage, choosing instead to live in a cohabitation arrangement without legalization? Is it because they fear that marriage imposes roles and expectations that stifle spontaneity in a relationship? Is it hesitation about commitment and permanence? Is it because of a fear of taking one another for granted? Is it a desire for a trial run before deciding on legal marriage? Certainly, all these reasons enter into cohabitation decisions.

Persons in a cohabitational arrangement are actually in a kind of "marriage"—as are a homosexual couple who share a residence in a committed relationship. Perhaps it's too simplistic to think any longer of marriage and singleness as two entirely separate entities. If we accept a sociological definition of marriage as consisting of an ongoing sexual and economic interdependence between persons who openly declare their relationship (at least to a limited public), then many cohabitants and gay couples are "married." It's as though there's a continuum stretching from "nonmarriage" on one side to "legal marriage" on the other. In between is a sociological definition of marriage, including trial marriage and ongoing cohabitation arrangements. Closer to the "legal marriage" side would be common-law marriage, which is legal in some states only. (For a fuller discussion, see Scanzoni and Scanzoni, 1981, chap. 8.) Homosexual unions also fit under the sociological definition; although at this writing, homosexual couples are not legally recognized in most states.

The question for religious leaders is, Where does a *theological* definition of marriage fit into all this? Should churches recognize cohabiting couples and gay couples as the equivalent of married couples? Should a ceremony or *religious* recognition of the covenant between the partners in such relationships be established even though they cannot or do not wish to have *legal* recognition? One minister, for example, writes of the plight of older widows and widowers who "sometimes wish for the community of faith to recognize their own love and covenant relationship" which, if it were legalized through formal marriage, would mean the cutting off of one or the other's pension which already provides inadequate income (Connor, 1980).

Sex and the Single Person

Separate from the cohabitation question, we need to face questions on sex and the single person in a religious context. Currently, more and more persons are choosing singleness as a lifestyle, although not necessarily for a lifetime. Young people are waiting longer to enter marriage. Also, many persons are single again as a result of divorce or the death of a spouse. Sexual expression is a real desire for large numbers of these persons. Many feel the religious community has failed them by being insensitive, judgmental, condemnatory, and by not providing realistic guidance. This is true in conservative Protestant churches as well as in mainline churches. The conservative *Christianity Today* magazine recently reported on a poll taken among 203 formerly marrieds in the singles group of a large evangelical church. All of the respondents described themselves as "born again Christians." Aware that church teachings upheld celibacy as the only option open to them while unmarried, only 47 percent of the divorced men and 24 percent of the women felt celibacy was realistic. The remainder either expressed uncertainty or a feeling that celibacy was unrealistic. Nevertheless, only 9 percent of the 57 men and 27 percent of the 146 women in the survey were actually celibate. The majority of both men and women felt tension between their faith and their behavior (Smith, 1979).

John Calvin, the primary theologian of Protestant Puritan thought, felt strongly that celibacy was a "gift of God" bestowed only on a few. Drawing upon Paul's statement that "it is better to marry than to burn," he felt that marriage was the only "remedy" capable of satisfying sexual desire. He felt that those who claimed God would help them in their struggles to be celibate were only fooling themselves. Calvin contended that God has already provided help by instituting marriage and persons are responsible to make use of this remedy rather than expecting some other help from God (*Institutes,* Book II, Chap. VIII, Section 42).

Most Protestant leaders would feel Calvin's advice is impractical for today. Certainly they are not ready to tell people to enter a marriage simply for a sexual outlet! Much more is expected of marriage. Moreover, Calvin's views do not account for the *divorced* person who has already gone through the pain of an unsatisfactory marriage and needs time and space before marrying again; it is also inadequate for teenagers who are now becoming sexually active at younger ages and in larger numbers. Nearly one-half of the unmarried teenage women between the ages of fifteen and nineteen are sexually active. And among unmarried young men aged seventeen to twenty-one, 70 percent report they have already had sexual intercourse (Kantner and Zelnik, 1980).

How can the religious community provide support to the sexually inexperienced teenagers who often report tremendous peer pressure to become sexually active? (This is also a problem for many formerly marrieds. "I believe and practice celibacy," reported one woman in the church survey mentioned earlier, "but in America in the 1970s I have to hide this fact *even* from church people" (in Smith, 1979, p. 917). And what part should the church play in encouraging contraceptive usage among those young people who choose to be sexually active?

These are only a few of the questions and issues facing Protestants today as we ponder human sexuality. Space prohibits listing others; they are many and complex. A head-in-the-sand attitude on the part of the religious community is unacceptable. Human beings have needs, fears, longings, and questions that require a response that (1) recognizes those needs and questions realistically and (2) is informed by spiritual values in dealing with them. The need for a theology of sexuality has never been greater!

BIBLIOGRAPHY

Berger, Peter L.; Luckmann, Thomas. *The Social Construction of Reality.* Garden City, NY: Doubleday Anchor Books Edition, 1967.

Bloesch, Donald G. *Essential of Evangelical Theology, Vol. I: God, Authority and Salvation.* San Francisco: Harper and Row, 1978.

Brown, Robert McAfee. *The Spirit of Protestantism.* New York: Oxford University Press, 1965.

Bryant, Anita. *The Anita Bryant Story.* Old Tappan, NJ: Fleming H. Revell Co., 1977.

Calvin, John. *Institutes of the Christian Religion.* Trans. by Henry Beveridge in 1945. Grand Rapids, Mich.: Wm. B. Eerdmans Publishing Co., 1957.

Conner, John T., "Let the Clergy Stop Signing Marriage Licenses." in *The Christian Century,* Vol. XCVII, No. 27, pp. 812-13. 1980.

Dayton, Donald, "The Social and Political Conservatism of Modern American Evangelicalism: A Preliminary Search for the Reasons." In the *Union Seminary Quarterly Review,* Vol. XXXII, No. 2, pp. 71-80. 1977.

Evangelicals Concerned, Inc., Various publications and newsletters. New York.

Feucht, Oscar E.; Coiner, Harry; Sauer Rohn, Alfred von; and Hansen, Paul. *Sex and the Church.* St. Louis: Concordia, 1961.

Fromm, Erich. *Escape from Freedom.* New York: Holt, Rinehart and Winston, 1941.
Furnish, Victor Paul. *The Moral Teaching of Paul.* Nashville: Abingdon, 1979.
Gardner, R. F. R. *Abortion: The Personal Dilemma.* Grand Rapids, Mich.: William B. Eerdmans Pub. Co., 1972.
Gusfield, J. R. Symbolic Crusade: *Status Politics and the American Temperance Movement.* Urbana: University of Illinois Press, 1963.
Jahr, Cliff. "Anita Bryant's Startling Reversal." In *Ladies Home Journal,* Vol. XCVII, No. 12, pp. 60-68. 1980.
Johnston, Robert K. *Evangelicals at an Impasse.* Atlanta: John Knox Press, 1979.
Kantner, John; Zelnik, Melvin. Report in Sept.-Oct. 1980 issue of *Family Planning Perspectives.*
Kennedy, David. *Birth Control in America: The Career of Margaret Sanger.* New Haven, Conn.: Yale University Press, 1970.
LaHaye, Tim; LaHaye, Beverly. *The Act of Marriage.* Grand Rapids, Mich.: Zondervan, 1972.
Landrum, Phil. "But What About Right Now?" In *Campus Life,* Vol. XXIX, No. 8, pp. 38-42.
Lyles, Jean Caffey. "Definitive Guidance for Presbyterians." In *The Christian Century,* Vol. XCV, No. 21, pp. 603-4. 1978.
Lyles, Jean Caffey. "The Presbyterian Family Reunion." In *The Christian Century,* Vol. XCV, No. 22, pp. 636-38. 1978.
Lyles, Jean Caffey. "The Other Evangelicals." In *The Christian Century,* Vol. XCVII, No. 33, pp. 1027-28. 1980.
Nelson, James B. *Embodiment: An Approach to Sexuality and Christian Theology.* Minneapolis: Augsburg Pub., 1978.
O'Neill, William L. *Divorce in the Progressive Era.* New Haven, Conn.: Yale University Press, 1976.
The Other Side: "The Gay Person's Lonely Search for Answers." Philadelphia, 1978.
The Other Side: "The Agony of Abortion." Philadelphia. 1980.
Page, Ann L.; Clelland, Donald A. "The Kanawha County Textbook Controversy: A Study of Politics of Life Style Concern." In *Social Forces,* Vol. 57, No. 1, pp. 265-81. 1978.
Pittenger, Norman W. *Making Sexuality Human.* Philadelphia: United Church Press, 1970.
Quebedeaux, Richard. *The Young Evangelicals.* New York: Harper and Row, 1974.
Quebedeaux, Richard. *The Wordly Evangelicals.* San Francisco: Harper and Row, 1978.
Scanzoni, John H. "A Sociological Perspective on Abortion and Sterilization." In *Birth Control and the Christian: A Protestant Symposium*

on the Control of Human Reproduction. Edited by Spitzer, Walter O.; Saylor, Carlyle L. Pp. 311-26. Wheaton, Ill.: Tyndale House Publ. 1969.

Scanzoni, Letha. *Sex is a Parent Affair.* Glendale, CA: Regal Books, 1973.

Scanzoni, Letha; Mollenkott, Virginia Ramey. *Is the Homosexual My Neighbor: Another Christian View.* San Francisco: Harper and Row, 1978.

Scanzoni, Letha,; Scanzoni, John. *Men, Women, and Change: A Sociology of Marriage and Family.* New York: McGraw-Hill, 1981.

Shedd, Charlie. *The Stork Is Dead.* Waco, Tex.: Word Books, 1978.

Sheppard, Gerald T. "Biblical Hermeneutics: The Academic Language of Evangelical Identity." In *Union Seminary Quarterly Review,* Vol. XXXII, No. 2, pp. 81-94. 1977.

Small, Dwight Hervey. *The Right to Remarry.* Old Tappan, NJ: Fleming H. Revell Co., 1975.

Smedes, Lewis. *Sex for Christians.* Grand Rapids, Mich.: Wm. B. Eerdmans Pub. Co., 1976.

Smith, Harold Ivan. "Sex and Singleness the Second Time Around." In *Christianity Today,* Vol. XXIII, No. 16, pp. 914-20. 1979.

Sojourners: "What Does It Mean to Be Pro-Life?" Washington, DC. 1980.

United Methodist Church, General Conference of. "Resolution on the Family." Nashville, 1976.

United Presbyterian Church, General Assembly of. Blue Book I, 190th Assembly of the United Presbyterian Church in the United States of America. San Diego, 1978.

Wink, Walter. "Biblical Perspectives on Homosexuality." In *The Christian Century,* Vol. XCVI, No. 36, pp. 1082-86. 1979.

Zurcher, Louis A., Jr.; Kirkpatrick, George R. *Citizens for Decency: Antipornography Crusades as Status Defense.* Austin: University of Texas Press, 1976.

Chapter Five
TOWARD A THEOLOGY OF HUMAN SEXUALITY

James B. Nelson, Ph.D.

The title of this presentation has some loaded words. Let me try to unpack some assumptions behind them.

"Toward a Theology of Human Sexuality." First, *toward*. The word intentionally suggests a direction and a tentativeness. Theology is a human enterprise; there are no final human answers to our fundamental questions, of which sexuality is surely one. The great theologian, Karl Barth, claimed that doing theology was like trying to paint a bird in flight. You can never capture the subject once and for all—it keeps moving.

Nevertheless, in spite of this necessary tentativeness, I do speak with personal conviction. I speak for myself—not on behalf of any particular faith group or religious institution. Indeed, as St. Mark counseled us (that was St. Mark Twain, a great American saint), the only persons who should be allowed to say "we believe" are the Pope, the King, and the person with tapeworms. The rest of us should speak for ourselves and say "I believe."

Second, the word *theology*. Literally, from the Greek words "theos" and "logos," it means the study of God, or more adequately, identifying the patterns of meaning about God and human life in light of God. For our purposes, we are looking at the meanings of human sexuality in light of faith in God as ultimate reality.

Next, *human.* Human sexuality. I assume that human sexuality is different from other animal sexuality. We share instinct and physiological drives and urges with other animals, but our sexuality is always more than that. It is a basic form of human communication. Like other animals, we communicate with those of our own species about feeding, mating, nesting, territory, and defense. But our communication virtually always expresses more than instinctual needs. We are forever telling each other what things mean to us in light of our own self-understandings and our understandings of the world. So also with human sexuality. Every sex act, every sexual expression is a communication of meaning of some sort.

Finally, *sexuality.* By "sexuality" I mean not only "sex"—physiological arousal and genital activity—that, too, but much more. Sexuality is a basic dimension of our personhood, not determining, but surely permeating all thought, feeling, and action. It is our self-understanding and way of being in the world as male or as female persons. It includes our sex-role understandings, our affectional orientations, and our capacities for sensuousness. It is our feelings about ourselves as *body*-selves, and our feelings about the body-selves of others.

So much for definitional assumptions. Now, since propositions of one sort or another are commonplace in sexual life, I want to make five propositions—proposals toward some fresh thinking and experiencing. I would like to see us move:

1. from theologies of human sexuality to sexual theologies,
2. from seeing sexuality as incidental to our experience of God to seeing it essential to that experience,
3. from viewing sexual sin as wrong sexual acts to understanding sexual sin as alienation from our divinely-intended sexuality,
4. from seeing religious salvation as antithetical to sexuality to the experience of "sexual salvation" as recovery of our wholeness as sexual beings, and
5. from viewing sexuality as incidental to the life of the religious community to understanding it as fundamental and intrinsic to religious community.

wrong. Sexual sin may, indeed, involve harmful sexual acts and expressions, but whatever it is, it surely goes deeper than that. Both Christian and Jewish theology at its best has long known that sin is not fundamentally acts, but it is fundamentally some sort of deep alienation—an alienation which then most likely results in harmful acts. But it is the alienation that is basic and causative.

We were created to be fully, beautifully, richly, affirmatively sexual people. Sin is alienation from that divinely-intended sexuality. To put it overly simply, sexual sin is not being too sexual—it is being not sexual enough.

If it is true that sin is always some kind of deep alienation, it is also true that alienation is always experienced three-dimensionally. When I am alienated, I am divided within myself, I am divided from my neighbor (or other creatures), and I am also separated from God. Think about sexual sin in that light.

Sexual sin is alienation from the self; it is division within. For one thing, the body becomes something other than the self. In some sense it is alien to the self. Even our language betrays this tendency. We talk about our bodies as objects, as possessions. "I have a body," we say, as if the body were a thing that the self (the ego? the spirit?) possessed.

The alienated body produces a mind detached from the depth of feelings. Lacking is my feel for the body's spontaneous rhythms. Lacking is an understanding of the body's meanings in its pain and pleasure. It has become a machine whose experiences and delights cannot be fully integrated into the self—and note well that this is the problem of both the Victorian and the hedonist (as different as they appear to be).

In addition, sexual alienation within the self is alienation from the neglected half of my intended fully-androgynous humanity. Males fear tenderness, vulnerability, and the depth of emotions. Females do not claim their strength, their assertiveness, their intellects. In sum, human beings live as half human.

But sexual sin is also alienation from the neighbor. What we reject within is projected outward. In the Middle Ages it was clear that the figure of the devil represented what people could not acknowledge in themselves. In the male it was the lustful Pan, and in the female the witch. In both, it was the magnified, distorted image of the erotic. But in our own less dramatic age we continue to project outward the alienation within. We distance ourselves in both emotions and bodies from our relationships, living much of our lives with calculated disembodiment—though athletes are given a temporary reprieve from such constraints under the goal post following the crucial play.

Alienation from the neighbor through sexual sin, however, is not just a matter of interpersonal relationships. We cannot understand much of the world's violence without understanding its connections to machismo, a hyper-masculinism of toughness, power, competition, and constant proving of oneself. We cannot understand white racism without knowing its sexual dimensions. And we cannot fathom our ecological dilemma without seeing how the dichotomy of spiritual and sensual has become the split between ourselves and the earth.

Basically, sexual sin is alienation from God. For a variety of reasons countless people have become convinced that in God's eyes human sexuality is a somewhat distasteful, regrettable necessity. Thus, early in Christian history the ideal of the ladder mysticism of late Greek thought became the goal. On the lower rungs of the ladder, the soul could love God through creatures, but on the highest rungs of the ladder (to which the truly religious must aspire) the soul loved God quite apart from any creaturely love. Thus, the soul becomes a solitary, uncontaminated virgin contemplating a God who is the same. And the body is pummelled so that the soul might be released.

While the individual histories of our sexual sin, our sexual alienation, are undoubtedly as complex and varied as each of us is unique; at the same time there are two common intertwining threads that bind all of our histories together: spiritualistic dualism and sexist dualism. Spiritualistic dualism has its roots in the body-spirit dichotomy contained in Greek culture at the beginning of the Christian era. Its ideal is the release of the eternal, pure spirit from the temporal, corruptible (and corrupt) body. It is "angelism"—the bodiless mind.

Sexist dualism, the other major thread of alienation, was present in the Old Testament culture well before the Christian era. This is "patriarchal dualism"—the systematic and systemic subordination of women in culture, institution, religion and interpersonal life.

The two dualisms intertwine in both history and personal life. In the alienation of spirit from body, of reason from emotions, of higher life from fleshly life, we have found both impetus and expression in the subordination of women. Men have assumed themselves superior in reason and spirit by identifying women with the traits of bodiliness, emotion, and sensuality. And while one sex bears the brunt of injustice, the humanity of both sexes is diminished.

Yet, in the eyes of faith sin is never the last word. Salvation is. Thus, the fourth proposition.

4. *I would like to see us move from viewing religious salvation as antithetical to sexuality, to the experience of "sexual salvation" as the recovery of our wholeness as sexual beings.* You do not need reminding of how many sincerely religious people in our society associate the notion of salvation with disembodiment, with becoming "pure spiritual beings" (whatever that is). Spiritualistic dualism continues to make its mark. But I am convinced that more authentic to the heart of both Christian and Jewish faiths is the claim that the experience of salvation here and now is the experience of sexual wholeness. Call it what you will—reconciliation, the possibility of new life, the resurrection of the body now—salvation embraces our sexuality and does not deny it.

It is important to me to reclaim and reinterpret the two historic and traditional terms used by Christians to point to the dynamics of salvation: justification by grace and sanctification by grace. Though the terms may strike some as hopeless pietistic jargon, I believe that they point to the dynamics of Cosmic Love which are both necessary and possible for human fulfillment.

First, justification by grace. A fitting contemporary translation of this is the human experience of radical, unconditional, unearned acceptance. Paul Tillich has evocatively put it this way:

> [Grace] strikes us when our disgust for our own being, our indifference, our weakness, our hostility, and our lack of direction and composure have become intolerable to us. It strikes us when, year after year, the longed-for perfection of life does not appear, when old compulsions reign within us as they have for decades, when despair destroys all joy and courage. Sometimes at that moment

a wave of light breaks into our darkness, and it is as though a voice were saying: "You are accepted. *You are accepted,* accepted by that which is greater than you, and the name of which you do not know. Do not ask for the name now; perhaps later you will do much.... *Simply accept the fact that you are accepted!*" If that happens to us, we experience grace. (Tillich, 1948, p. 162)

When we have experienced that kind of acceptance, even momentarily, we know that everything is different. And what if we take seriously the possibility that this radical acceptance by the heart of the universe is addressed to the total and sexual self—and not to a disembodied spirit? Then we might extend Tillich's language something like this: You are accepted, the total sexual you. Your body, which you often reject, is accepted by that which is greater than you. Your sexual feelings and unfulfilled yearnings are accepted. You are accepted in your attempts at sexual purity, and also in your hedonistic irresponsibility. You are accepted in your sexual fantasies which both delight and disturb you. You are accepted in your femininity and in your masculinity, and you have elements of both. You are accepted in your heterosexuality and in your homosexuality, and you have elements of both. Simply accept the fact that you are accepted as a sexual being. When that happens to you, you experience grace.

To affirm and to celebrate God's radically accepting love does not require us to engage in a romanticized idealism about the possibilities of human perfection. Nevertheless, in those moments when we are open to the cosmic acceptance, in some measure everything *is* transformed. If the old fears, dualisms, and alienations do return (as perhaps they will), still, we are not the same as before.

This affirmation leads to the second dynamic of salvation: sanctification. That traditional word also needs rehabilitation. For too many people it has meant growth in a kind of holiness that is anti-sexual. But what if we were to take seriously the possibility that God's gracious empowerment both intends and enables our increasing sexual wholeness and fulfillment? If so, I suspect that sexual sanctification might mean several things.

Sanctification means self-acceptance, self-love. True, Christian piety has not had a very good record of dealing positively with self-love, but we are learning that we cannot love anybody or anything very well unless we also have a fundamental self-love. And such capacity to accept ourselves deeply without false pride, without glossing over our own brokenness, is truly a gracious gift. Self-acceptance personalizes the body, making us aware of the roots of our tensions, pains, joys, nurtures the spontaneity of the body-self. Self-acceptance brings with it a profound sense that I can celebrate the body which I am, and thus celebrate the ways in which my body-self relates to the world. It is a resurrection of the body.

Sanctification of our sexuality thus also means sensuousness—growth in the capacity for sensuousness. It is the sensuousness of the Song of Solomon in the Old Testament, a marvelous Hebrew love poem celebrating the joys of erotic communion. Such love poetry is carnal knowledge. It is a hymn to the beauty of bodily existence and the sheer joy of God's creation as an erotic garden. In such sensuousness the body becomes a means of grace, and the graceful forms of the body are a means of love. We need to remember that the affirmation of sensuality is not an inherently dangerous invitation to mechanical hedonism. Actually, the inner dynamic seems to be quite the opposite: the unloving suppression of the self's eros eventually nurtures depersonalized bodies, be they those of the Victorian or the libertine.

If sanctification means greater sensuousness, it also means an increased capacity for self-transcendence. In the peak of sexual excitement during intercourse, orgasmic pleasure can reach the heights of ecstasy in which I feel taken out of myself. Yet, at the same time my body-self feels profoundly unified and I feel intensely myself. This, surely, is a part of sexual sanctification. It is the renewal of the capacity for play, the recovery of the child within me. It is the diffusion of the erotic throughout my entire body, not the narrowing of sexual focus to the genitals alone. And with the resexualization of my body comes the eroticization of the world, so that the environment takes on its deliciously sensuous qualities which we have previously forgotten.

Thus, sexual sanctification means growth in sexual freedom. I am not talking about license here, but rather the kind of thing Abraham Maslow spoke of, when reflecting on the sexuality of "self-actualizing people." By self-actualizing, he meant that these people were secure in their sense of self-worth and had the capacities to accept and give love. And what was their sexual freedom? They enjoyed genital sex more fully than most people, yet specific sex acts were not central to their lives. The sex act itself seemed to range widely in its capacity to evoke feelings—from the mystically ecstatic, to the sheer sense of fun and play. Their talk about sex was considerably more free, more casual, and less conventional than the average person's. They recognized their sexual attraction to others, yet were less driven to secretive affairs precisely because their own committed relationships were so satisfying. They made no really sharp differentiation between the roles and personalities of the two sexes. They possessed a sense of well-being, of merriment, of elation. They seemed to have an unusual ability to affirm the other's individuality and were committed to the growth of others and themselves. Now, all of these characteristics to which Maslow pointed, seem to be quite a remarkable portrait of freedom and responsivness in sexual expression. That kind of freedom, it appears to me, is a humanizing freedom, and it depends upon a deep sense of personal worth and a capacity for trust. Religiously speaking, that means grace—sanctifying grace.

And, of course, sexual sanctification means the possibility of growth in androgyny. No one of us is humanly destined to be either rational or emotional, either assertive or receptive, either cognitive or intuitive, either initiating or nurturing, either strong or vulnerable, but all of these. The ancient Greeks knew that their gods Apollo and Dionysus belonged together, Apollo personifying detachment and objectivity and Dionysus personifying proximity and union. The two were equally honored in the high temple in Delphi. We do not have to *become* androgynous, however, for each of us essentially *is*. We only need to be allowed to be actually what we are essentially. And that kind of permission comes from a sense of security, a security which in religious terms is grace.

Any human salvation as we know it, including our sexual salvation, is partial and incomplete. Yet it can be real. True, the unhealed, unreconciled parts of our sexuality will continue to hurt us and others. But the first and last word of faith is the gracious love of the Cosmic Lover experienced as radical acceptance and as empowerment for greater wholeness. The Word is made flesh, and our flesh is confirmed.

This leads to my fifth and last proposition:

5. *I would like us to move from viewing sexuality as incidental to the life of the religious community to understanding it as fundamental and intrinsic to the religious community.* Once again I remind you that I speak from a Protestant Christian standpoint, though I hope with some relevance to the Catholic and Jewish communions. My point in this fifth thesis is simply that recognition that the religious community itself as a sexual group (among other things) will assist us, in the words of the old song, to accentuate the positive and eliminate the negative.

One thing this will mean is a greater attention to resexualizing our theology. By this I do not mean putting sexuality into a theology from which it has been absent—it has always been there. I just mean a new level of consciousness about the ways in which our sexuality, for both good and ill, has shaped our expressions of faith.

A basic example is the Judeo-Christian understanding of God. Stereotypically, masculine language and images have helped shape that understanding. It has been masculine pronouns: God is "he" and "him." But also masculine titles: Lord, Master, King, Father. But also a masculine imagery and spirituality which has emphasized God as structure, law, judgment, intellect, logic, and order. Thus the experience of only one gender has dominated our perceptions of God.

Yet, one of the best kept secrets in the Old Testament is the abundance of feminine images for God. God is there likened to the woman laboring in childbirth, giving birth to a new creation; God is seen as nursing mother and as a seamstress clothing her children. And what would a more feminine-shaped spirituality look like? Perhaps nature would be accented more than society, mystical oneness more than cognitive analysis, immanence more than transcendence, flow and change more than structure. These dimensions of the God experience we need, and a more inclusive, androgynous theology will help us.

If the church really understands itself as a sexual community, then, the lives of its participants can be enhanced, not only in theology and doctrine, but in its worship and liturgy as well. The two sacraments commonly observed by Protestants are evident. In infant baptism, for example, although the primary theological symbolism is that of the child's acceptance of God's gracious love, there is more. The birth of the infant is celebrated (surely a sexual event), as is the sexual relationship of the parents who transmitted new life. And when adults are baptized by immersion, the water enfolds the body not only like the grave from which new life is symbolically risen, but also like the womb out of which new life is born. The eucharist or sacrament of communion with its elements of bread and wine symbolizing body and blood is preeminently a sacrament of body theology: "This is my body given for you."

To the extent that participants in these sacraments can be aware of their sexual dimensions, to that extent they can also be helped to understand how human sexual experience itself can be sacramental. By "sacramental" here I mean simply those acts or occasions in which the presence of God is experienced with particular vividness and life-giving qualities. And in this sense I believe that good sexual love-making can be richly sacramental and with some intriguing parallels to the formal sacraments of the church. Like baptism, a loving act of sexual intercourse is a reenactment of dying and rising. The French knew what they were doing in calling orgasm "the little death," for there is a temporary loss of self-conscious individuality in sexual climax. But with this comes the self's death in surrender to the other, and then the self is received back with new life, joyful and replenished from the divine plenitude itself.

With the sacrament of communion there are also parallels to sexual intercourse. The eucharist's body language is obvious. And its promised unity is not a unification which erases the individuality of the participants, but rather a communion through which unique individuals intimately and deeply touch the lives of each other. The appropriate mood for the eucharist is one of joy, expectancy, and gratitude. And there is a futuristic promise present, for the sacrament is an earthly experience of the ultimate unity promised to everyone in the New Age. Every one of these things about the church's sacrament of communion is true also of good, honest, sexual love-making.

There are, of course, dangers in pointing to these parallels. One is the possible implication that sexual intercourse is automatically sacramental. Of course it is not, but neither is there anything mechanical or automatic or magical about Christian sacraments. Without genuine participation in their meaning and significance, these liturgical rites are either meaningless of potentially detrimental to the participants. And this of course is true of genital sex. But my point is this: sexual love *does* have the capacity to break the self open not only to deep communion with another person, but also to the life-giving presence of God. Again and again in sex countless people experience the secret of human wholeness and the authentic meaning of divine grace. And if this is true, by labeling the experience for what it is and by religiously celebrating it, its power can be enhanced.

The other danger is the possible implication that insofar as sexual lovemaking is sacramental it is destined to be pious, terribly serious, and somewhat dull. Are playfulness, eroticism and lusty fun to be banished in the name of God? By no means! It is tragic that so much religious piety has been so stereotypically "holy"—and dull. The more authentic point of it all is that the life-giving presence of the Cosmic Lover meets us in every mood of loving eroticism. When the religious community is affirmed as a sexual community, these possibilities will become more evident to us.

Now, I offer one final illustration of the sexual dimensions of religious community: the commitment of church and synagogue to social justice. There are, obviously, a variety of justice issues which are clearly sex-related. Among them are: economic and political justice for women and gays, the abortion question, prostitution, pornography, rape and wife battering, the sexual protection of minors, the sexual well-being of those in institutions, over-population—the list could go on. But I would argue that a wholistic vision of human sexuality can help the religious community to see more clearly and respond more effectively to important sexual dimensions in vast social issues which, at first glance, seem to have little to do with sexuality.

Think of social violence. Blessed are the peacemakers? We will not be effective peacemakers until we recognize and cope more adequately with the sexual dimensions of crime on the streets or the insanity of a global arms race. The links of such violence to a machismo image of masculinity with its cult of competitiveness, its prizing of toughness and superiority, its demand for potency, and its homophobia are simply too basic. Further, the links between deprivation of body pleasure and tendencies toward physical violence are compelling.

Think of white racism in America. We will not cope with it adequately until we label and deal with the deep sexual dimensions of racism—the ways in which schizophrenic male attitudes toward women were organized along racial lines and the white male guilt projected onto the black male who was then fantasized as a dark sexual beast, or the ways in which the disembodied insecurity of white people with their own flesh can lead us to the dirty body image of those who are so obviously different from us.

Think of the ecological dilemmas which threaten the human future. It is no accident that we almost instinctively use sexual language here—speaking of "the rape of the earth" or longing to recapture a St. Francis vision of sexual kinship with nature ("Brother Cloud and Sister Moon"). Just as our bodies are ourselves and not simply things to be used by the self, so also we are part of the earth. Too long we have treated the earth with a pornographic sensibility—like a prostitute to be mounted with lust and then rejected with loathing when we are through with her. It is time to reach toward an erotic sensibility wherein the earth is affectionately caressed and lovingly embraced as beloved partner. When the religious community realizes how much it is also sexual community, when it can affirm more celebratively the sacramentality of sex, then we might also more fully capture the vision of an erotic and a sacramental world.

All I have been trying to suggest in these pieces of a sexual theology is put into perspective by the French philosopher Paul Ricoeur (Ricoeur, 1971, pp. 13–ff.). He observed three major stages in the evolution of Western understandings of sexuality in relation to religion. The earliest stage identified the two realms. Sexuality was incorporated into the believer's total understanding of reality through patterns of myth, ritual, and symbol.

Then, noted Ricoeur, when the great religions arose during the second stage, there came a separation. Now the sacred was experienced as transcendent, untouchable, separate—heavenly and not earthly. The meanings of sexuality were demythologized and limited to a small part of the total order, essentially that of procreation within the institution of marriage. The power of sexuality was feared and condemned; it was to be restrained by strict discipline.

A third period is now emerging, however. It is marked by the concern to release once again "the lyricism of life" in uniting sexuality with the experience of the sacred and of the cosmic order. This period is marked by: more wholistic understandings of the person, by more insights into the ways in which sexuality is present in the total range of human experience, and by the recognition that sexuality is so involved in the center of a person's life and creative potential that its denial thwarts the richest possibilities of human fulfillment.

I believe we are entering that third period. Because I am neither Pope nor King nor (to my knowledge) do I have tapeworms, I can speak only for myself. But I urge the explorations and visionings of us all, with some confidence that (as T. S. Eliot once put it)

> We shall not cease from exploration
> And the end of all our exploring
> Will be to arrive where we started
> And know the place for the first time.
> (Eliot, 1952, p. 145)

BIBLIOGRAPHY

Elaboration of each of these themes may be found in my book *Embodiment: An Approach to Sexuality and Christian Theology*. Minneapolis: Augsburg Publishing House, 1978.

Tillich, Paul. *The Shaking of the Foundations*, p. 162. New York: Scribners, 1948.

Ricoeur, Paul. "Wonder, Eroticism, and Enigma." In *Sexuality and Identity*, edited by Hendrik M. Ruitenbeek, pp. 13-ff. New York: Dell, 1971.

Eliot, T. S. "Four Quartets: Little Gidding." In *The Complete Poems and Plays, 1909-1950*, p. 145. New York: Harcourt, Brace, 1952.

Chapter Six
AFTERWORD

William Simon, Ph.D.

The views in this afterword are shaped by a self-conscious secularism, as close to the "death of God" position as one can be who has grown up in and shared this culture's many legends of demons, sorcerers and fairies, sharing the same legacy of fantasy and anxiety. My perspective shares with Freud the view that theologies are essentially regressive responses to many of the most basic aspects of human existence. They are regressive in the sense of being organized by immature or archaic perceptions and solutions and thus, are closed to alternative perceptions and solutions.

The three "survey" essays provide an image of contemporary religion, meanwhile carrying an enormous burden of judgments initially fashioned in worlds profoundly remote to contemporary reality. As a whole, the four essays present implicitly a history of western conceptions of god and present a history of the ways in which Western religions have viewed the sexual. It begins with the angry tribal god of ancient Judaism (a god capable of saying that "I will smite them unto the seventh generation" to an audience so tied to collective identities that they were incapable of asking what the second through seventh generation might have done to merit such attention); next came the gods of the Reformation who now appear in the guise of moral bookkeeper and pragmatic entrepreneur (the moral life being the surest route in an uncertain world to success now and salvation later). More recently, god appears as a humane, if not humanistic psychotherapist (a god capable not only of bringing an empathetic understanding to the sins we commit, but who extends that understanding to the sins we imagine we commit).

Missing in most of this is a recognition that the very conditions that contributed to both our changing conception of god and the religiously mandated proscriptions and prescriptions regarding the sexual may have also changed the very nature of the sexual. The slowly changing character of the human body contributes to the image of the sexual as being some kind of transcendent constant that links the current moment to that remote antiquity that serves as the point of origin for so much of our shared religious imagery. Concepts of organs and orifices, seen as sexual, have changed over history as well as the nature of the sexual experience. For theology—conservative, moderate, or liberal—the sexual apparently has defined its meanings with little regard for the specific processes of psychosexual development as it occurs in given socio-historical contexts.

The furthest away from concerns for existential realities (the realities within which our most basic sense of the erotic is formulated) are the traditional or conservative theologies that credit to the sexual some primary uses, that reflect divine architecture; then, they define the sexually appropriate and inappropriate in terms of the logic of those uses. Typically these center around procreative responsibilities and consequences. The moderate to liberal positions are only slightly different. They tend to begin with some empirically unexamined assumptions about our sexual natures and, at their best, appear more humane by arguing the need to accommodate our moral standards to a more "realistic" understanding of those sexual natures. These empirical understandings, more often than not, involve the introduction of other uses of the sexual, uses that may be as remote to our developmentally acquired capacity for eroticism as those mandated by the more traditional views. Indeed, liberal theologies suggest uses of the sexual—love, communication, and respect for personhood (regardless of how the latter is defined)—that may be significantly more difficult to achieve than those required by the traditional attitudes. Why do sexual passions and sexual moralities seem so difficult to reconcile?

Perhaps the greatest disservice to humanity that theology and the social sciences (the latter being something of a secular theology, invoking their own god-terms to justify what are more often than not moral judgments) propose is an image of woman and man that serves to alienate women and men from their own experiences of themselves. Or worse, it provides a vocabulary of meanings for those sexual experiences that often invoke feelings of guilt, anxiety, and self-hatred. For example, requiring the sexual (in its acceptable forms) to be the necessary companion of love may be no less alienating than making sex the necessary companion of species, community, or family survival. The very circumstances that make the concept of personhood possible, the stable integration of love and desire, may be as difficult as it is attractive.

An acknowledgment of the sexual at the existential level—which neither theology nor social science have done to any considerable extent—requires us to ask, what evokes sexual desires? And, distinct from desire, what evokes sexual arousal? What produces sexual pleasure? Lastly, what affords sexual satisfaction? The answers to these questions, although undoubtedly interrelated, finds each reserving territories and significances all their own.

Human collectives have defined and organized the sexual in a wide variety of ways, as against the relative uniformities of the human as a biological entity. This suggests that the above questions cannot be found in the biological itself, except, somewhat ironically, on the most abstract levels.

Theologies tend to view the sexual in universal terms—phylogenetically rather than ontogentically—and thus avoid seeing it as being critically shaped (if not created) by the experiences of specific individuals with specific sociohistoric contexts. To do so would not only require that theologies confront the specific processes through which our individual erotic cultures are fashioned, but also to see the role religion and religious symbols play in shaping such erotic cultures.

There are two questions that set a focus for us. Firstly, can religion survive without the sexual? Or, why must this aspect of human behavior be singled out for a quality of moral significance rarely accorded other forms of behavior?) Secondly, can the sexual, as the contemporary western world knows it, survive without religion? Foucault and other have suggested that the Puritan tradition, although appearing to suppress the sexual in all but its most minimal forms of expression, actually served to elevate the sexual to virtually unprecedented levels of significance for both individuals and communities. As a result, individuals may have engaged in less sexual *behavior,* and engaged in more sexual *conduct* as both the behavior and non-behavior became charged with potential sexual significance. The sexual, by definition, was infused with a moral significance that related directly not only to acts, but to character and worth.

I suspect that the sexual takes on an exceptional significance for theologies, largely because of its essentially non-exceptional character. It becomes exceptional because it is an aspect of human behavior that all individuals must confront, and in doing so are capable of experiencing themselves as engaging a moral universe. What else can an ordinary individual do without extraordinary requirements or risk and still outrage the religious community and possibly even a god? (To explore the potential for either demonstrated evil or virtue in other aspects of human behavior would threaten the survival of either the community or the church. Clearly, if theologies were to demand behavior and expose motives in the areas of commerce or politics, and scrutinize with equally powerful moral mandates, such theologies would promptly be charged as being either irrelevant, subversive, or both.) Even the secular view of the sexual is seen as extraordinary moments in the life of the human; it all contributes to the impulse to draw the blinds, to lower the lights, and to experience *the act* with an uncharacteristic and sometimes terrifying silence. This generalized view depends upon the cultural legacy of the sexual as the original (if not ultimate) sin for the belief in our own capacities for evil or ecstasy. In other words, the theological new transforms and inflates the meaning of the sexual. The sexual returns to the religions a powerful salience that it can claim in few other aspects of human behavior. Much of liberal theology, like that offered by Nelson, persists in believing that the promise of ecstasy can survive without the threat of evil, or that the joy of control can be effectively replaced by the control of joy.

So I ask: can the churches exist without sex? They seem unable to recruit by organizing societies and communities. Success in recruiting by family tradition is declining. How does the church saliently touch our lives? Whether dealing with the repressive requirements of traditional theology or the utopianism of liberal theology, religion shows little promise of abandoning the special and over-burdened role it assigns to human sexuality.

But are we not all—or nearly all—compliant in preserving this over-burdening of the sexual? Therefore, another question: can sex survive without religion? In our book *Sexual Conduct,* John Gagnon and I attempt to distinguish between sexual *behavior* (or the occurrence of an act defined as sexual) and sexual *conduct* (the evaluating meaning or significance of the behavior). These two dimensions of the sexual can vary independently of one another. For example, the prostitute engages in sex often and experiences very little of it as sexually extraordinary, whereas the client generally may have sex rarely with a prostitute and is more likely to experience this activity as extraordinary.

I suspect that most of human history on this planet to date could be illustrated as a world where sex was not engaged in very often and was not considered very important. There are a few known examples of societies where sex occurs with relatively high frequency and where it is not viewed as a matter of great moral significance. Much of the modern western experience has been a case of fairly restricted levels of sex behavior, and this behavior takes on potentially extraordinary significance. Much of this can be attributed to the Puritan tradition and its child, the romantic tradition, which promised—and sometimes demanded—that love and lust could coincide. In a sexual utopia (from some points of view), both frequency and significance should occur at high levels. But is this only utopian, or merely the inevitable outcome of the western experience? I wonder if we can begin to find ways of metaphorically enriching the sexual that are more "cost effective" in their ability to yield pleasure and satisfaction which are richer than their potential for guilt and anguish. Or, perhaps we can consider moving towards views of the sexual that deflate its present significance, even at the risk of lessening its ability to provide easy rituals of intimacy.

Nevertheless, much of what previously looked like progress within the worlds of theology, with its increasing liberal—if not liberated—view of the sexual, now looks as if it has merely shifted our attention to a more attractive part of the swamp.

BIBLIOGRAPHY

Foucault, M. *The History of Sexuality, Vol 1, An Introduction.* Translated from the French by Robert Huxley. New York, Pantheon Books, 1978.

Gagnon, J. and Simon, W. *Sexual Conduct: The Social Sources of Human Sexuality.* Chicago: Aldine Press, 1973.

an invitation to join
The Association of Sexologists (T.A.O.S.)

. . . a membership association which evolved from discussions with those concerned with reflecting and best-serving the multi-disciplinary needs of the human sexuality field:

OUR GOALS

- to encourage and support the study and practice of the professional field of sexology.
- to provide a support network for sexologists and others interested in areas relating to human sexuality.
- to be a central source for sexological information, experience, training and service.
- to serve as an advocate for sexologists and their causes.
- to provide a forum for research and development in the field, and an opportunity for professionals to learn from other fields and update needed skills.

Our Horizons and Potentials are Unlimited
We Need You and Want Your Support

Life Member		$500.00
Member/Sexologist . Annual Dues		50.00
Friend of T.A.O.S. . Annual Dues		50.00
Student Member . . Annual Dues		25.00

For further information, write:

The Association of Sexologists
1523 Franklin Street
San Francisco, CA 94109

Telephone:
(415) 441-7078